GEOMETRY

CONSTRUCTIONS AND TRANSFORMATIONS

Iris Mack Dayoub

Model Secondary School for the Deaf

Gallaudet College

Washington, D.C.

Johnny W. Lott

University of Montana

Missoula, Montana

DALE SEYMOUR PUBLICATIONS

Copyright © 1977 by Dale Seymour Publications.
All rights reserved. Printed in the United States of America.
Published simultaneously in Canada.

Order number DS01022
ISBN 0-86651-499-6
(Previously published as ISBN 0-88488-175-X)

DALE
SEYMOUR
PUBLICATIONS
P.O. BOX 1088
PALO ALTO, CA 94303

4 5 6 7 8 9 10 -ML- 99 98 97

CONTENTS

CHAPTER TWO

TRANSFORMATIONS

NOTATIONS

Terms and notation which may be new to students are explained in the exercises. Some of the notation used without explanation follows:

$\overleftrightarrow{AB}$ denotes the *line* determined by points A and B.

$\overline{AB}$ denotes the *segment* with endpoints A and B.

AB denotes the *length* of $\overline{AB}$; that is, AB is a *number*.

$\overrightarrow{AB}$ refers to the *ray* with endpoint A and containing B.

∠ XYZ refers to the *angle* formed by $\overrightarrow{YX}$ and $\overrightarrow{YZ}$; or if there is no chance of confusion, it may be denoted by ∠ Y.

m∠XYZ denotes the *measure* of ∠XYZ; that is, m∠XYZ is a *number*.

m⊥p indicates that lines m and p are *perpendicular*.

m‖p indicates that lines m and p are *parallel*.

⊙ P denotes a *circle* with center P.

PREFACE

A LETTER TO THE STUDENT

We want to help make the study of geometry enjoyable, and we want to offer something different. If you are just beginning to study geometry, we think the exercises in this book will help make geometry meaningful. For those of you who want a fresh approach to geometry, the transformations we use should make the study of geometry more interesting.

You will need a Mira to do many of the problems in this book. If you have used the Euclidean tools, compass and straightedge, to perform constructions, you will probably find that the Mira is easier to use and more fun.

A LETTER TO THE TEACHER

We think that one should begin to learn geometry at the concrete stage and move gradually to an abstract level. Much has been written lately about the excessive formality and rigor in high school mathematics programs. Most educators agree that somehow we have lost sight of the role intuition plays in the development of mathematical knowledge. This book was written for teachers who want to give students the opportunity to use their intuition.

There are at least two types of geometry problems which encourage students to use their intuition. One asks the student to do a certain construction, make some observations, then form a conjecture. Another asks the student to analyze properties of a familiar geometric figure in order to make a certain construction.

The construction required for problems of either type can be accomplished quickly and accurately with a device called a Mira. The geometric tool, a transparent plastic reflector, was invented by George Scroggie and N. J. Gillespie and is available through corporations that sell mathematics education materials in the United States and Canada. Standard constructions are quickly and accurately made with the Mira. The Mira is more than equivalent to the compass and straightedge; that is, the Mira can be used to perform constructions which are not possible with straightedge and compass. For example, with the Mira any angle can be trisected.

This book can be used with a traditional geometry course or a course in transformation geometry. The constructions of Chapter One can be integrated into the curriculum or used to introduce various topics of the course. The solutions given to the constructions are in no way unique. Given the opportunity, the student will discover his own constructions, and in attempting to justify the methods used in the constructions, will begin to learn the nature of proof. The use of the Mira as a discovery aid often prompts the student to take the next step and make deductive conclusions. While the students are learning to construct geometric figures with a Mira, they will often discover important properties of the figures.

Many textbooks which take a transformation approach to geometry are too abstract for students since most students do not intuitively know what an image under a translation or rotation looks like in terms of two reflections. A student's first experiences should be in actually sliding and turning sets of points to locate translations and rotation images. The exercises in Chapter Two lead the student from his intuitive notions of translation and rotation as a slide and turn, to the notion of translation and rotation as the composite of two reflections. The exercises demonstrate that there are exactly four isometries. Size transformations and isometries are used to introduce the concept of similarity. Using the Mira with the exercises in this book brings concreteness to the abstract concepts of transformations.

CHAPTER ONE

CONSTRUCTIONS

All of the problems in this chapter can be solved with a Mira. When you first get your Mira you should play, explore, and experiment with it. Use pairs of coins, buttons, dice, and other objects to try to fit one object into the image of a similar object. Use your Mira to make designs and to copy pictures. Be sure to look at a cloudy sky through the Mira.

For best results, the Mira should be used on a flat surface in a well-lit room. A sharp pencil is vital when drawing the Mira line, marking image points, and drawing figures.

EXERCISE 1.1

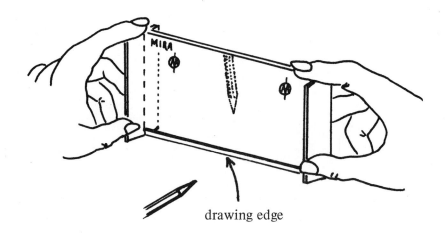

drawing edge

Hold the Mira on your desk as shown in the Illustration.

In this position the Mira's drawing edge will be touching the desk and will also be facing
  you.

Notice that the drawing edge is set back a little behind the face of the Mira.

Place your Mira on this page so that its drawing edge lies along m.

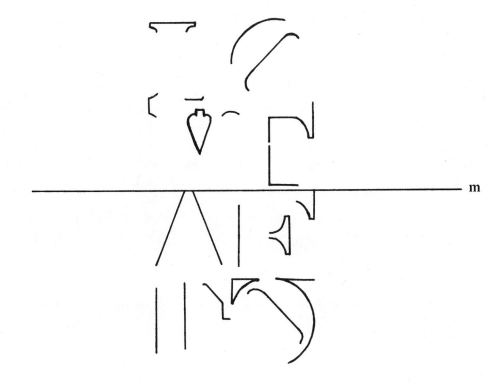

2

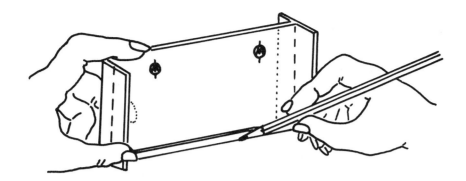

In the illustration a student is drawing a Mira line. Notice how he holds the Mira steady
with one hand and traces along the drawing edge with the other. This tracing is called
a Mira line.

Adjust the position of your Mira so that the image of the point P maps onto the point Q.
Is the drawing edge facing you?

Hold the Mira firmly in this position and trace along the drawing edge. Be sure to use a
sharp pencil.

Q is said to be the "image of P" or "P is reflected onto Q."

Locate the image Y of X in the Mira line you have drawn.

Q·

·X

·P

Simple Simon wanted to save money by building only one pump house P by the stream
and running a pipe line to his barn B and to his house H. He felt sure that a pipe line
making ∠HPB a right angle would be the shortest distance. Simon had a good idea,
but it is not necessarily the shortest distance. Can you find the short cut?

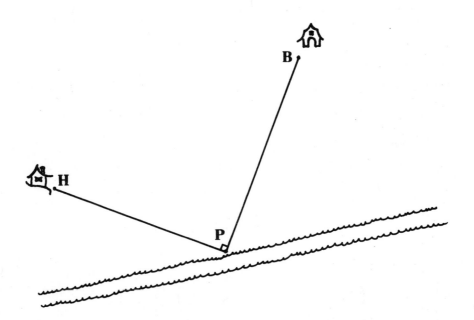

EXERCISE 1.4

Place the drawing edge of your Mira along m. Notice that s is reflected onto itself. Lines m and s are perpendicular (m⊥s).

Locate A′ the Mira image of A over m; then draw the line $\overleftrightarrow{AA'}$. How are $\overleftrightarrow{AA'}$ and m related? How are $\overleftrightarrow{AA'}$ and s related?

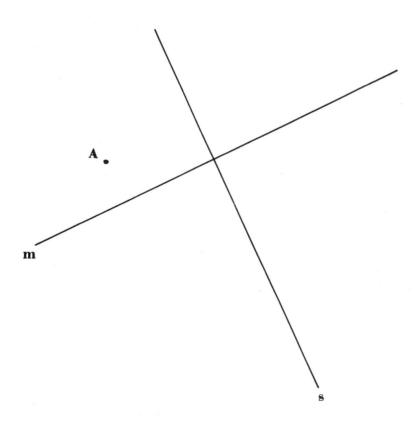

EXERCISE 1.5

Draw a line m through A that is perpendicular to s.

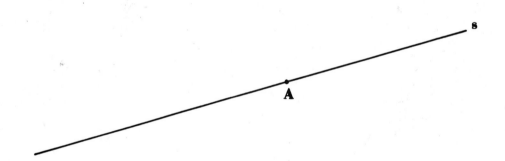

Draw a line m through B perpendicular to s.

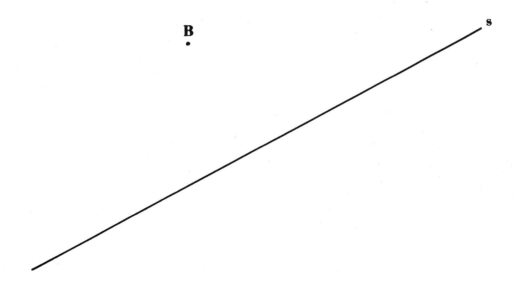

Draw the perpendicular bisector of $\overline{AB}$.

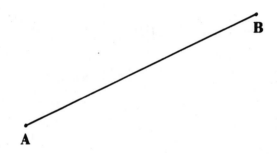

Find a point A on circle C and a point B on circle D so that m is the perpendicular bisector of $\overline{AB}$.

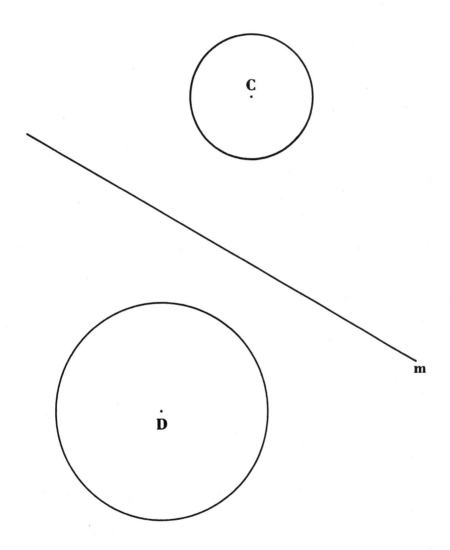

EXERCISE 1.9

Bisect ∠XYZ.

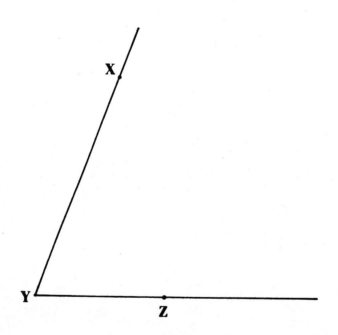

EXERCISE 1.10

Locate points A, B, and C so that m∠AOD = 90°, m∠BOD = 45°, and m∠COD = 22½°.

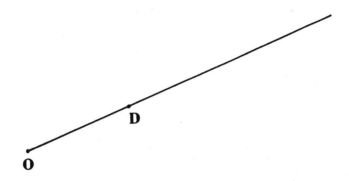

Find a line n so that n is the bisector of the angle formed by p and m. Line n is called the midline of p and m.

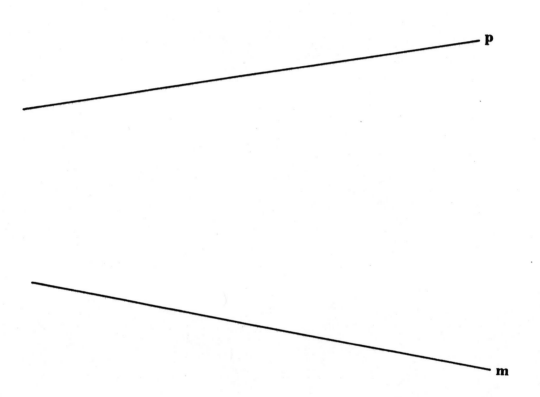

EXERCISE 1.12

Find the midline n of p and m. Use your Mira to show p∥m∥n.

———————————————————————— p

———————————————————————— m

Locate points A′ and B′ on p so that AB = A′B′.

Locate a point E on p so that DC = EC.

Locate a point X on m so that XY = AB.

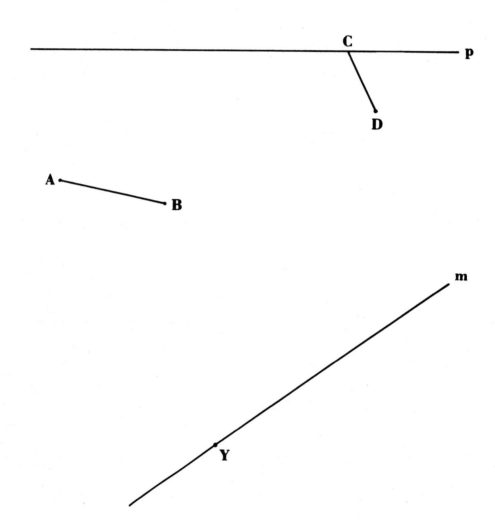

EXERCISE 1.14

Copy ∠MNO so that its vertex is at A and one side of the angle is on p.

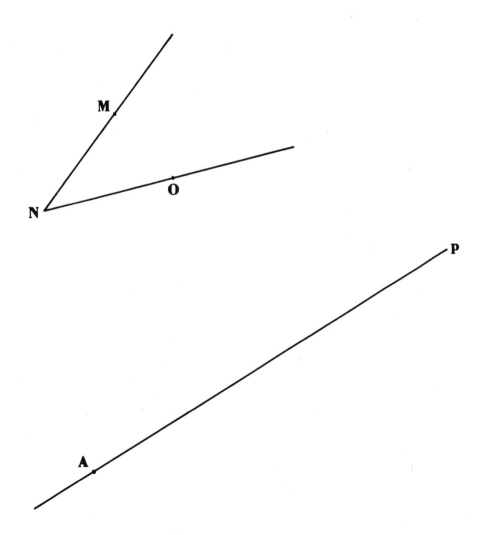

EXERCISE 1.15

Draw a line m through A so that m is parallel to s.

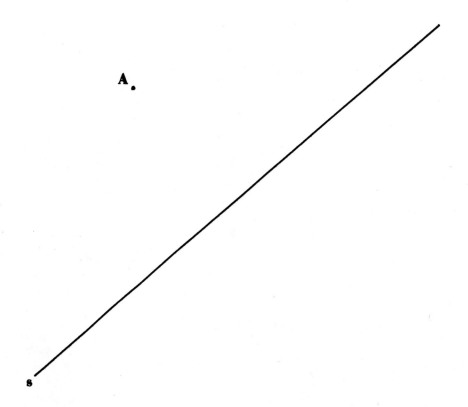

Locate the point S so that PQRS is a parallelogram.

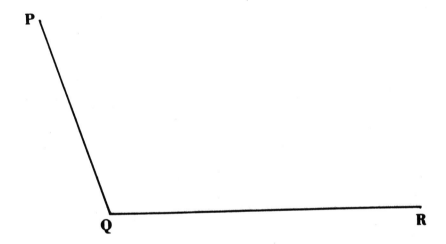

EXERCISE 1.17

Find all segments that have one endpoint on q, one endpoint on ⊙O, and that have P as midpoint.

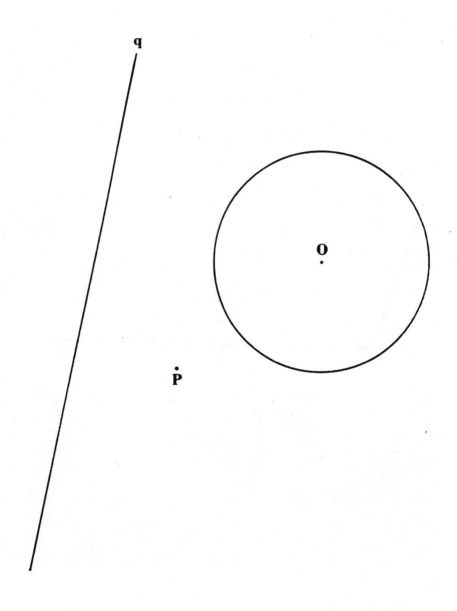

EXERCISE 1.18

Locate points X on p and Y on q so that $\overline{XY}$ is parallel and congruent to $\overline{AB}$.

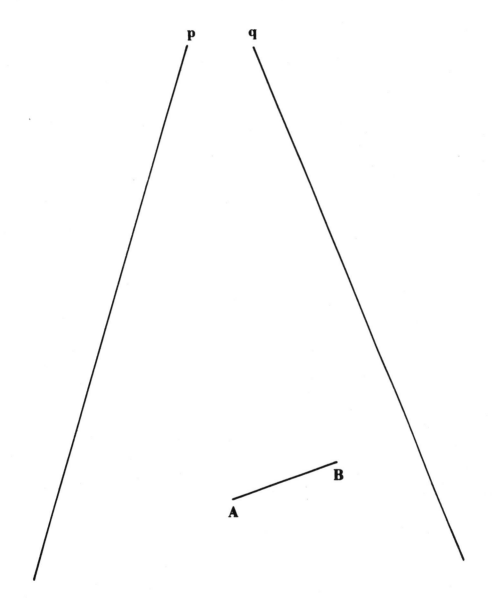

Locate points C and D so that ABCD is a square.

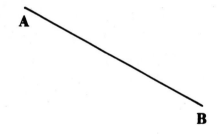

Inscribe a square in this circle.

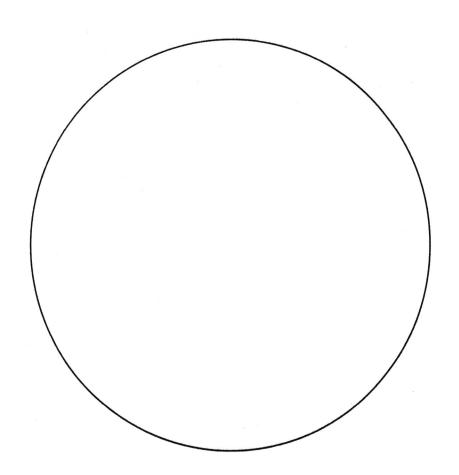

EXERCISE 1.21

Find a square AXDY with X and Y on q, D on ⊙F, and A on ⊙E.

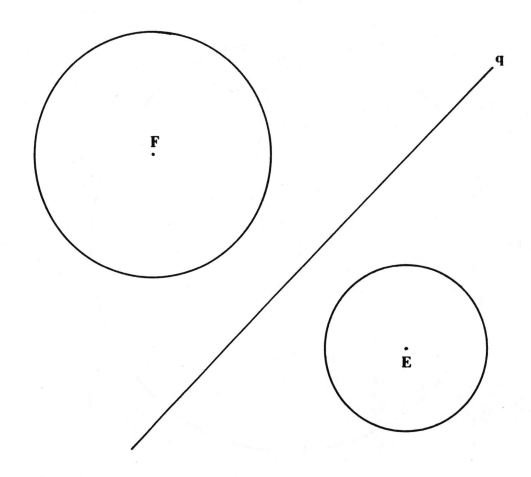

EXERCISE 1.22

Draw an isosceles right triangle XYZ so that XY=YZ.

Z _____ Y

Find a point R so that △PQR is an isosceles right triangle with right angle at R.

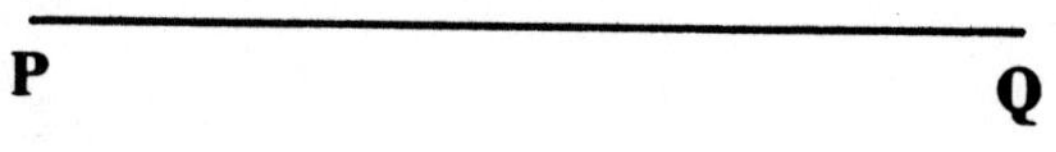

P ——————————————————————— Q

EXERCISE 1.24

Locate points C, D, E, F, G, and H so that ABCDEFGH is a regular octagon.

A ———————————— B

Draw a segment of length $\sqrt{(AB)^2 + (BC)^2}$.

Draw a segment of length $\sqrt{|(AB)^2 - (BC)^2|}$.

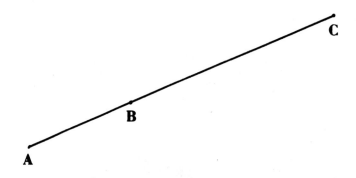

EXERCISE 1.26

Locate the points on this number line that correspond to the numbers $\sqrt{2}$, $\sqrt{3}$, $\sqrt{4}$, $\sqrt{5}$, $\sqrt{6}$.

Divide $\overline{AB}$ into five congruent segments.

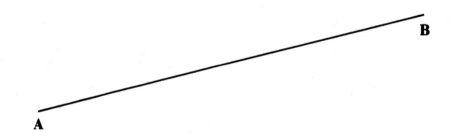

EXERCISE 1.28

Construct a segment whose length x is the mean proportional to the lengths a and b; that is, so that $\frac{a}{x} = \frac{x}{b}$.

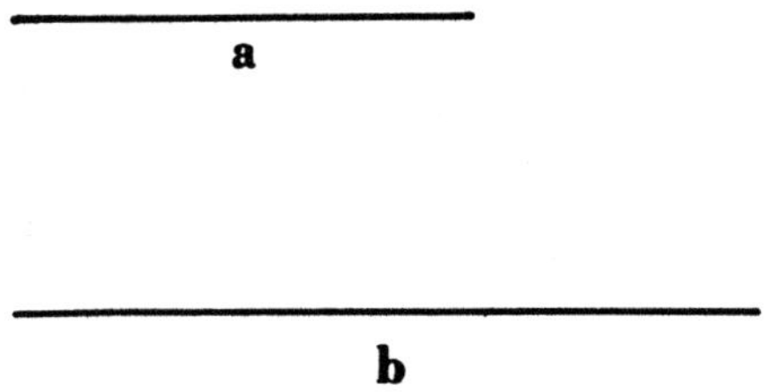

_____
a

_____
b

Draw a rectangle whose sides have length x and y and so that one side of the rectangle is on m.

Construct a rhombus on m that has an angle with measure a and sides of length x.

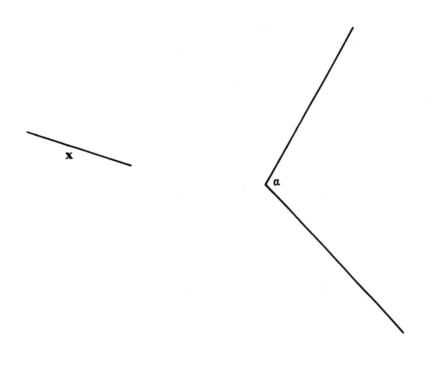

Draw parallelogram PQRS so that m∠QRS = β, PQ = XY, and PS = XZ.

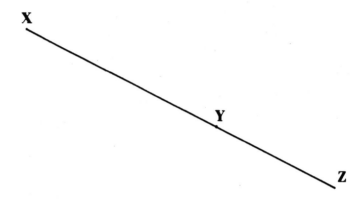

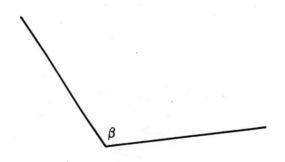

EXERCISE 1.32

Draw the bisectors of the angles of the triangle below.

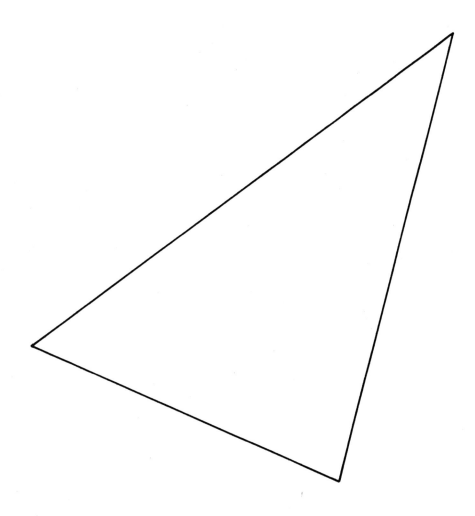

Inscribe a circle in this triangle.

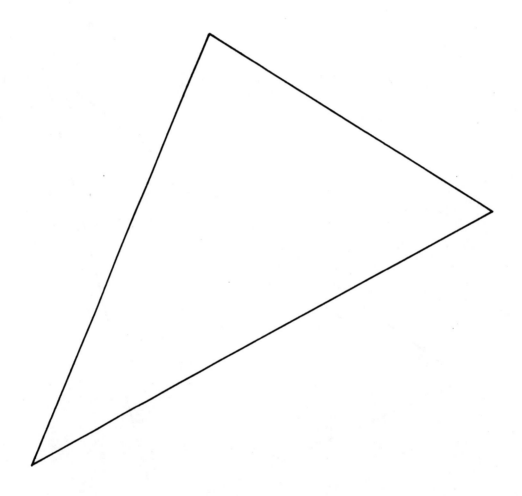

EXERCISE 1.34

With your Mira locate the center and radius of the circle that is tangent to each of these lines.

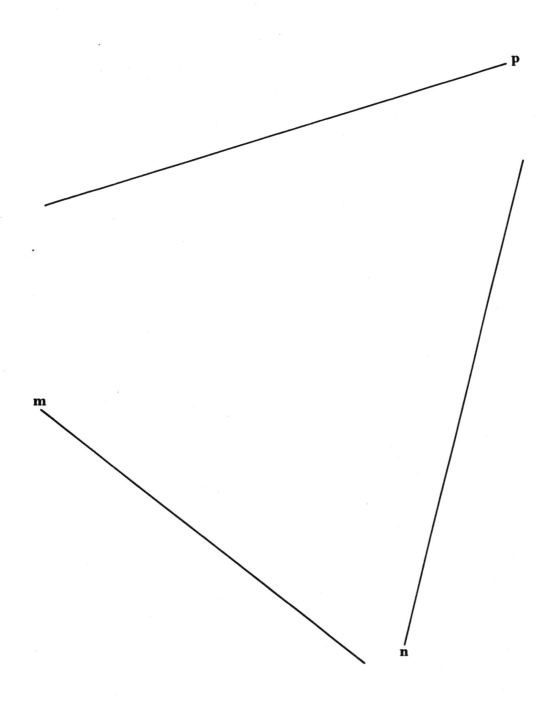

Draw the bisectors of the interior and exterior angles of this triangle.

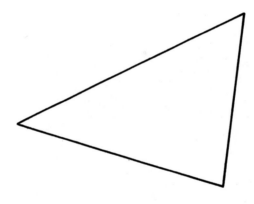

Label the points of tangency of the incircle of △ ABC.

Draw the lines through each vertex and the point of tangency of the opposite side.

The point of concurrency of these lines is called the Gergonne point, after J.D. Gergonne (1771-1859).

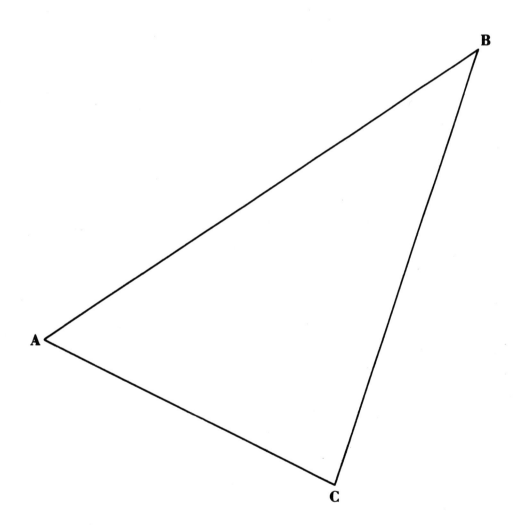

EXERCISE 1.37

Draw the lines containing the altitudes of each triangle.

Make a conjecture about the location of the orthocenter, the point at which the lines
containing the altitudes of a triangle are concurrent.

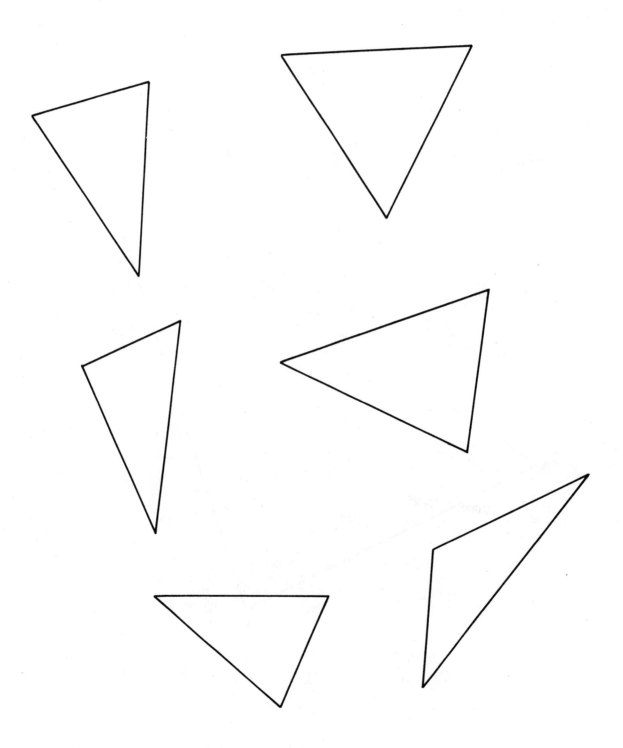

Draw the perpendicular bisectors of the sides of these triangles.

Make a conjecture about the location of the circumcenter, the point at which the perpendicular bisectors meet.

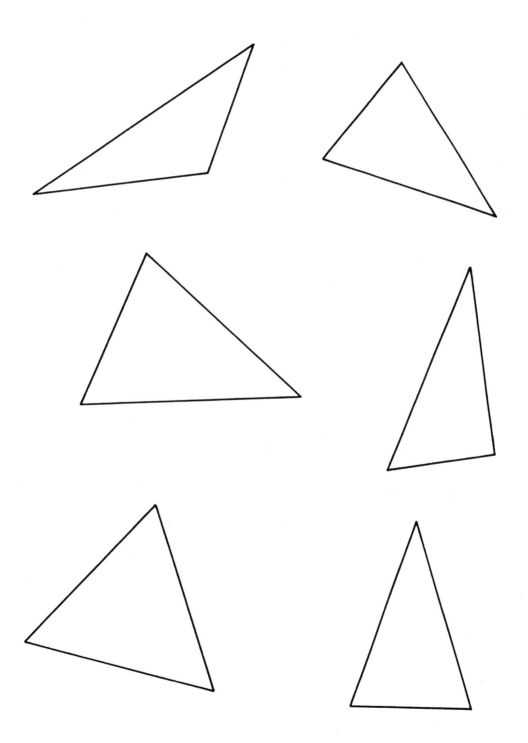

EXERCISE 1.39

Use your Mira to locate the center of the circumcircle of this triangle. Then draw the circle with a compass.

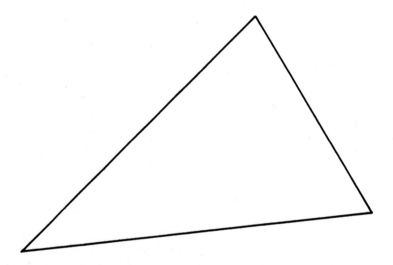

Drop perpendiculars to the sides of the triangle from any point P of its circumcircle. Draw a line through the feet of the perpendiculars. This line is called the Simson line of the point P, named for the Scottish mathematician Robert Simson (1687-1768).

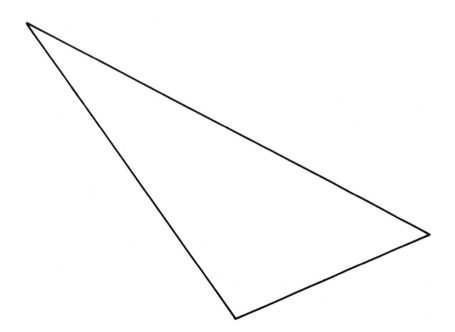

Find the point P whose Simson line is parallel to m.

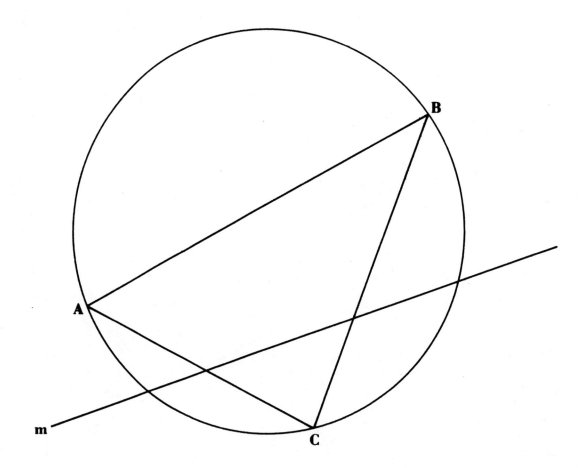

EXERCISE 1.42

Draw the medians of the triangle. The segment joining a vertex of a triangle to the midpoint of the opposite side is a median of the triangle.

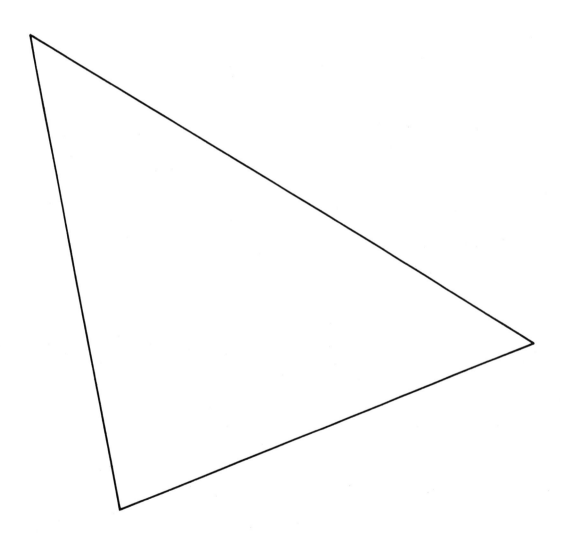

Use your Mira to find the orthocenter H, circumcenter O, and centroid M of △ ABC.

The line through these points is called the Euler line, for Leonard Euler, a Swiss mathematician (1707-1783).

Compare OM and MH.

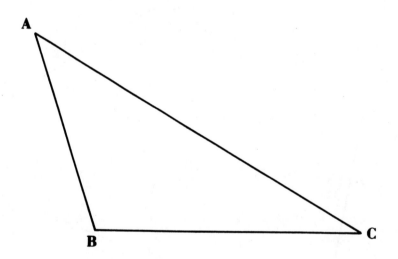

EXERCISE 1.44

The Feuerbach circle (also called the nine-point circle) of a triangle contains the midpoints of the sides, the feet of the altitudes, and the midpoints of the segments from the orthocenter to the vertices of the triangle.

The center of this circle is the midpoint of the segment joining the orthocenter and the circumcenter of the triangle. This point is called the Feuerbach point.

This theorem is due to K.W. Feuerbach, a German mathematician (1800-1834).

Draw the Feuerbach circle for △ABC.

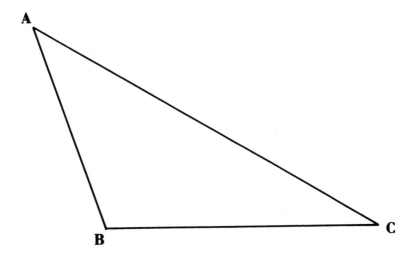

Use your Mira to locate a point C so that △ABC is equilateral.

Draw an inscribed equilateral triangle.

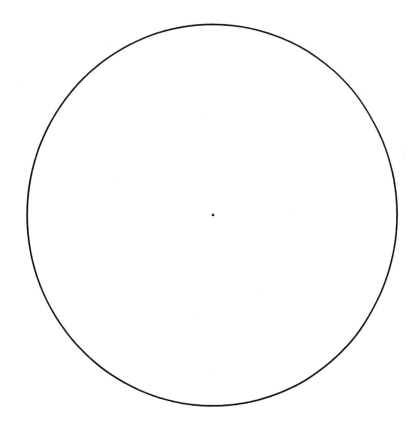

Without drawing diameters, locate 6 equally spaced points on the circle.

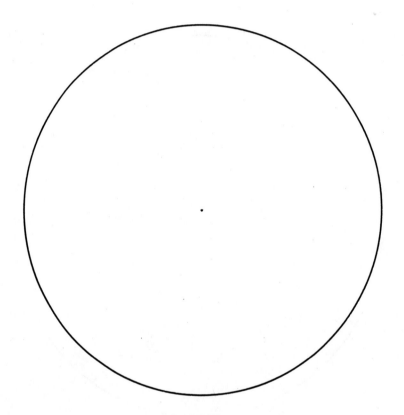

EXERCISE 1.48

Locate points P, Q, and R, each on one of the three concentric circles so that PQR is an equilateral triangle.

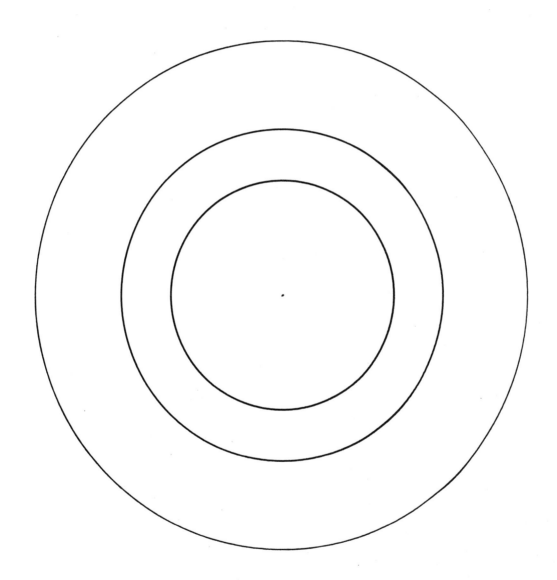

Locate a point S so that $\overline{SV}$ is the hypotenuse of right triangle STV and SV = 2(VT).

$$\overline{\hspace{6cm}}$$

V   **T**

Use your Mira to find a point J so that $\overline{JK}$ is the hypotenuse of right $\triangle JKL$ and
JK = 2(JL).

K   L

Locate points U, V, and W so that

m∠XOU = 60°

m∠XOV = 30°

m∠XOW = 15°

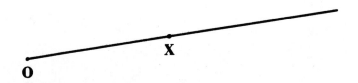

EXERCISE 1.52

Lines a, b, and c are parallel. Use your Mira to find two points, P on line a and R on line c, so that $\triangle$PQR is an equilateral triangle.

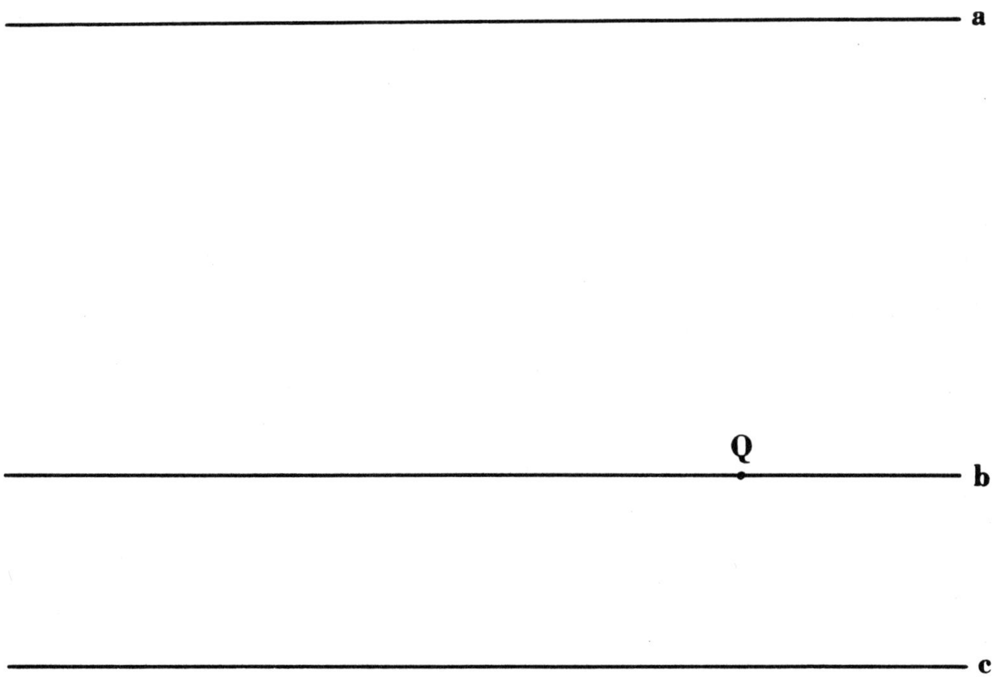

———————————————————————————— a

Q
————————————————————•———— b

———————————————————————————— c

Trisect ∠XOY.

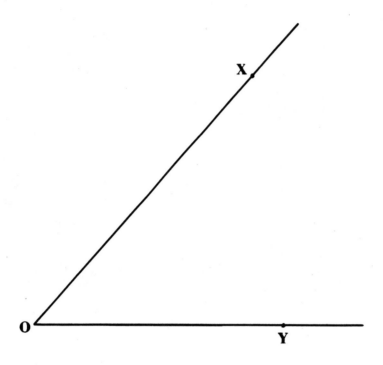

Choose a point P on $\overrightarrow{OX}$ and locate a point S on $\overrightarrow{OX}$ so that OP = PS.

Through P draw the line n parallel to $\overline{OY}$ and draw the line m perpendicular to $\overline{OY}$.

Find the Mira line that reflects S onto m and reflects n through O. Locate R the image of O.

m∠XOR = 2(m∠ROY).

The idea for this construction is due to Pappus (ca. 300 A.D.)

Trisect ∠PQR.

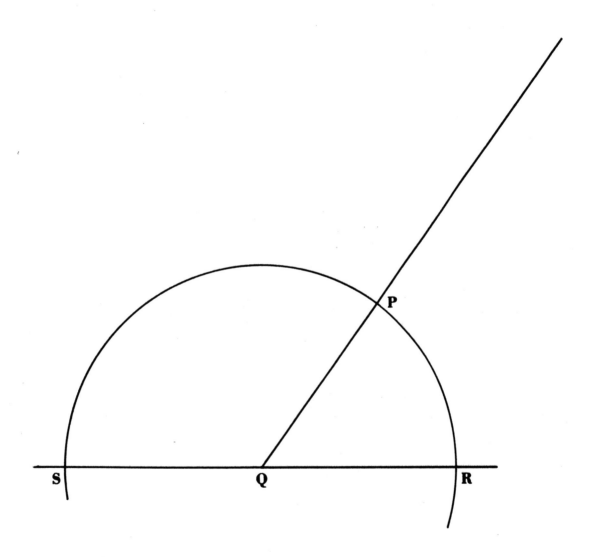

Find a Mira line that reflects Q onto $\widehat{PR}$ and S onto $\overrightarrow{QP}$.

If Q′ is the image of Q, then m∠RQQ′ = 2(m∠PQQ′).

Find the Mira line m that reflects R onto $\overrightarrow{QP}$ and reflects Q onto $\overset{\frown}{SP}$.

Let R' denote the image of R, Q'' the image of Q.

Let $Q' = \overset{\frown}{PR} \cap m$.

From the previous exercise you know that $\overrightarrow{QQ''}$ trisects $\angle SQP$;

Show that $\overrightarrow{QQ'}$ trisects $\angle PQR$. What can you say about $\triangle Q''Q'Q$?

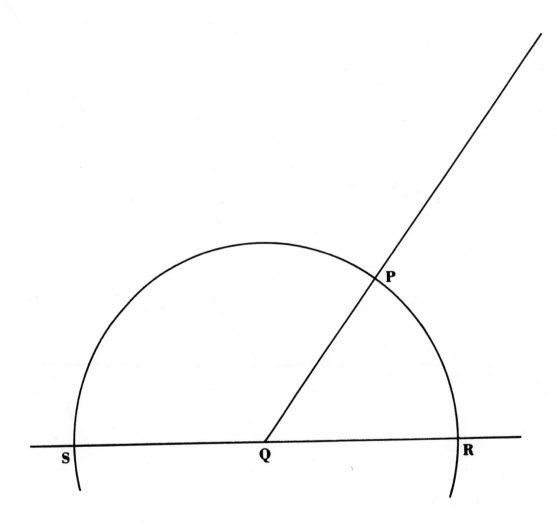

Divide this circle into nine congruent parts.

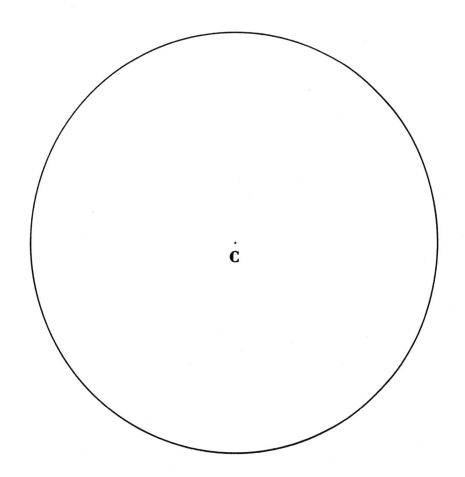

Locate points C, D, E, F, G, H, and I so that ABCDEFGHI is a regular nonagon.

A   **B**

Locate points C, D, and E so that ABCDE is a regular pentagon.

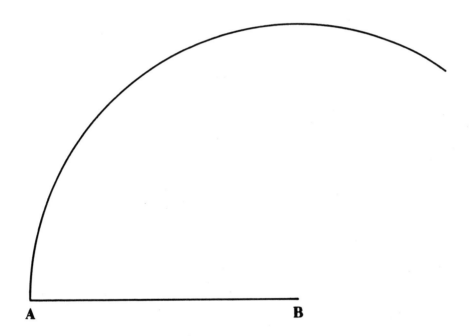

Draw m the perpendicular bisector of $\overline{AB}$.

Find a Mira line that reflects A onto m and B onto ⊙B.

Then C is the image of B, and D is the image of A.

Using m as a Mira line, locate E.

EXERCISE 1.59

Find an angle with measure 1° by trisecting a 3° angle.

Hint: Refer to Exercise 1.58 to draw a 72° angle and to

Exercise 1.51 to draw a 60° angle.

3 = 18 - 15 = ¼(72) - ¼(60).

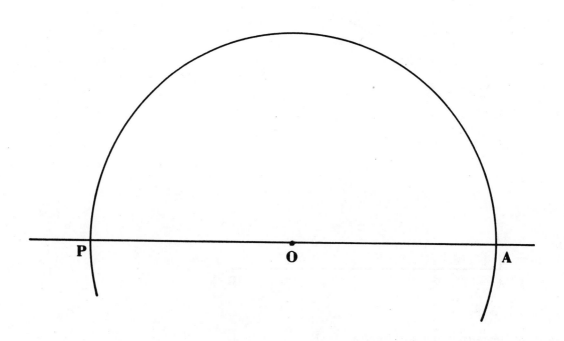

EXERCISE 1.60

Divide this circle into five congruent parts.

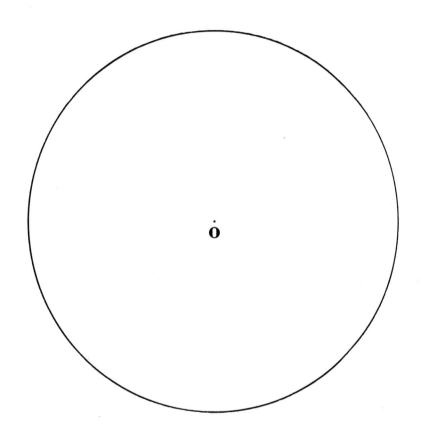

Let $\overline{PQ}$ be a diameter of circle O.

Construct radius $\overline{OR} \perp \overline{PQ}$.

Locate X the midpoint of $\overline{OQ}$.

Find the point R′ so that R′ $\in \overrightarrow{XP}$ and XR′ = XR.

Each side of the regular pentagon inscribed in circle O will have length RR′.

Note: This construction is due to Eudoxus (408-355 B.C.) who also showed that each side
of the regular decagon inscribed in circle O will have length R′O.

Locate the center of this circle.

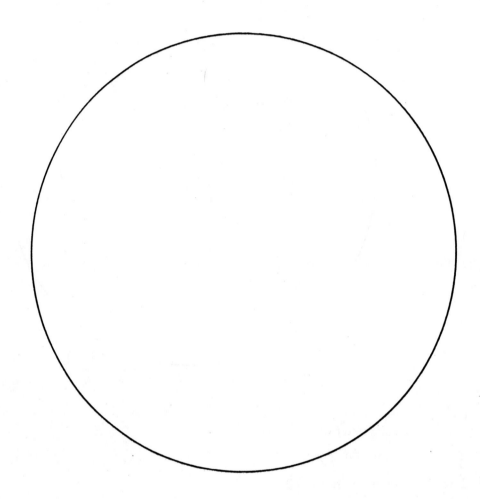

EXERCISE 1.62

Find the midpoint M of the given arc and locate the center C of the circle that contains

the arc.

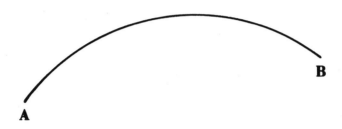

EXERCISE 1.63

The points K, J, and L determine a circle since they are not collinear. Locate the center of this circle and without using a compass to draw the circle, locate two or three additional points of the circle.

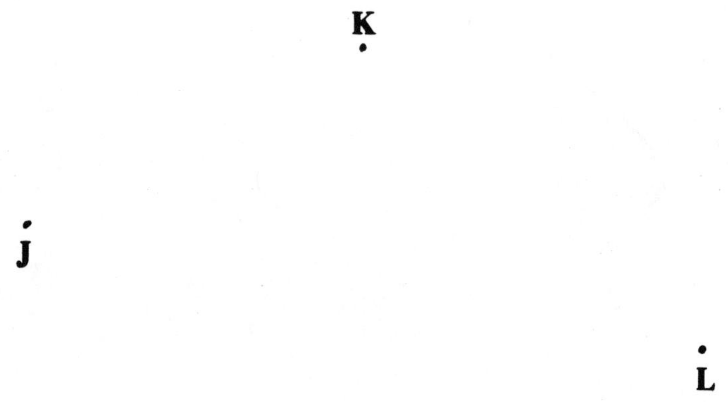

K
.

J
.

.
L

EXERCISE 1.64

Without using a compass, locate a point D so that ABCD is a cyclic quadrilateral with

$\overline{AD} \parallel \overline{BC}$.

A polygon is cyclic if the vertices of the polygon determine a circle.

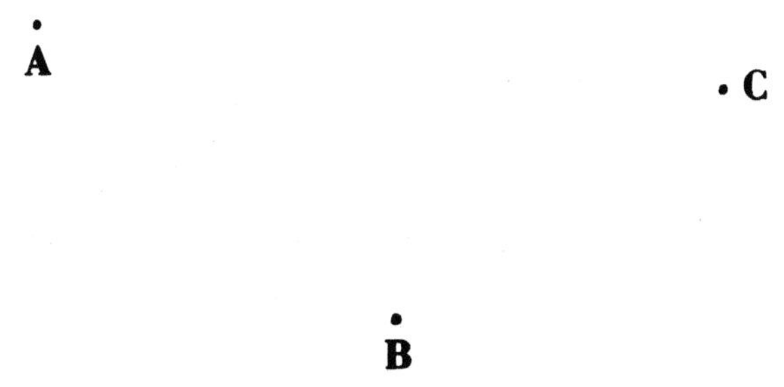

$\overset{\cdot}{\mathbf{A}}$

$\cdot\,\mathbf{C}$

$\overset{\cdot}{\mathbf{B}}$

EXERCISE 1.65

Draw the tangent t to the circle through A.

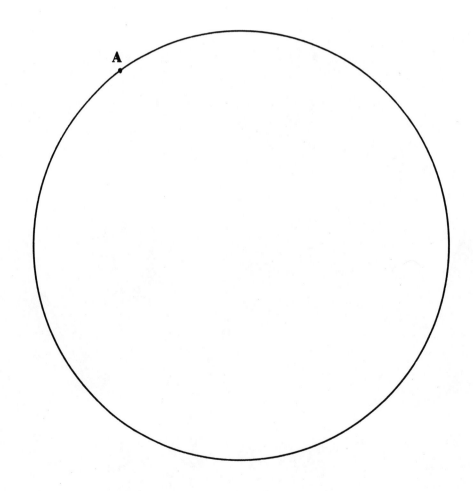

Construct the tangents to circle O that contain the point B.

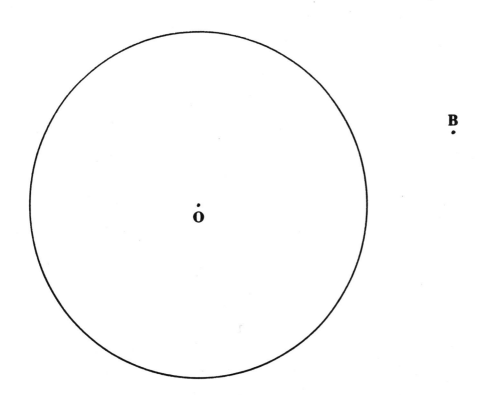

EXERCISE 1.67

Locate points D, E, F, and G on $\overrightarrow{AB}$ so that $\dfrac{x}{y} = \dfrac{AD}{DB} = \dfrac{AE}{AB} = \dfrac{AB}{AF} = \dfrac{AB}{BG}$.

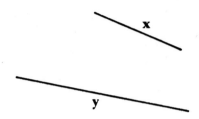

A •————————————————————• B

EXERCISE 1.68

Find the common tangents to these circles.

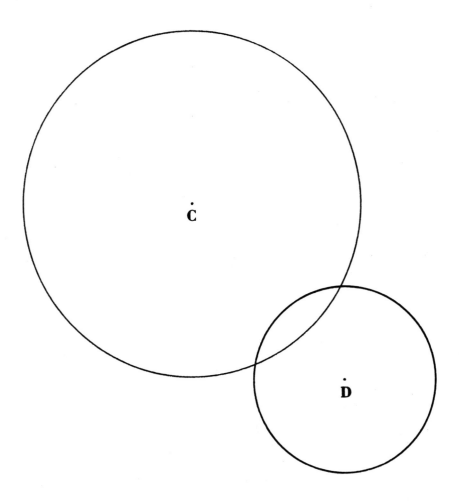

Hint: If the common tangent intersects

$\overleftrightarrow{CD}$ at M, then $\dfrac{CM}{DM} = \dfrac{\text{radius } \odot C}{\text{radius } \odot D}$

Using a Mira line through the midpoint of $\overline{AB}$ locate E the image of B on $\overleftrightarrow{RS}$. Draw $\overline{AE}$ and $\overline{BE}$, and let X and T be the points where these segments intersect the circles. What can you conclude about $\overleftrightarrow{XT}$?

The idea for this construction is due to Archimedes (ca. 287-212 B.C.).

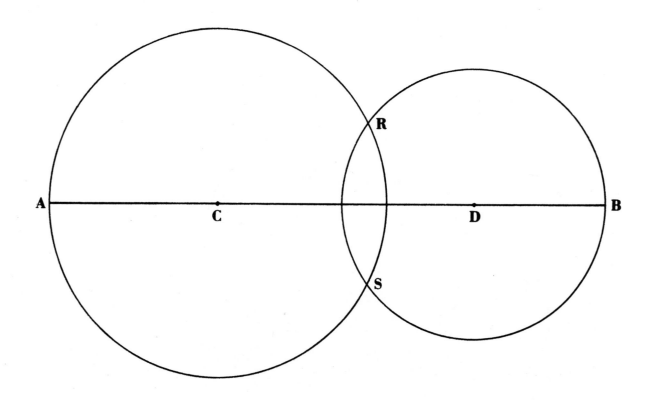

Try this construction for two externally tangent circles where $\overleftrightarrow{RS}$ is the common internal tangent.

Can you find a line to use for two externally disjoint circles?

EXERCISE 1.70

Find the common tangents to these circles.

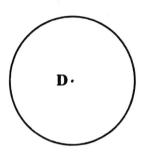

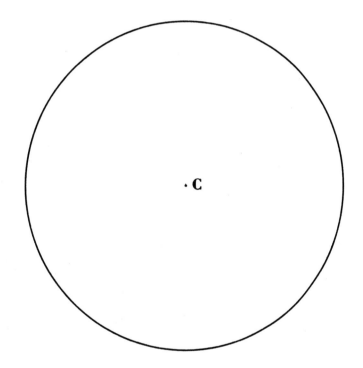

Hint: For the common internal tangent, locate N on $\overline{CD}$

so that $\dfrac{CN}{ND} = \dfrac{\text{radius } \odot C}{\text{radius } \odot D}$

For the common external tangents locate the point M as in Exercise 1.68.

Draw the tangents to the circle that are parallel to m.

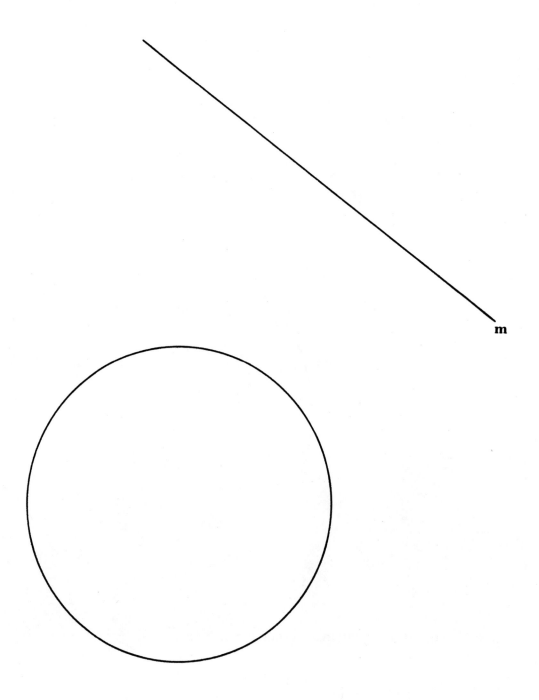

EXERCISE 1.72

Use your Mira to locate the center of the circle that is congruent to ⊙D and externally

tangent to ⊙C at A; then draw the circle with a compass.

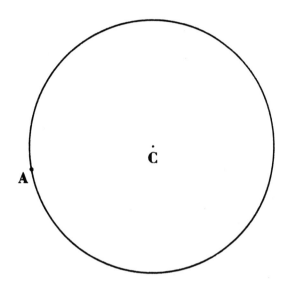

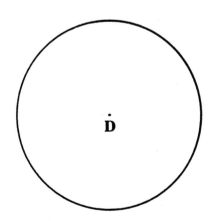

Find points B′ and C′ so that ⊙B ≅ ⊙B′, ⊙C′ ≅ ⊙C, and so that ⊙A, ⊙B′, ⊙C′ are pairwise externally tangent.

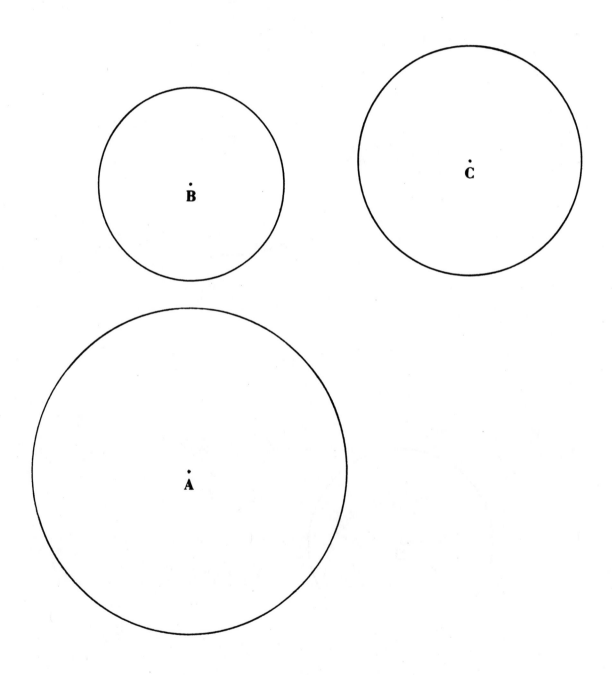

EXERCISE 1.74

Use your Mira to locate the center E of a circle that is congruent to circle D and is tangent to both m and circle C.

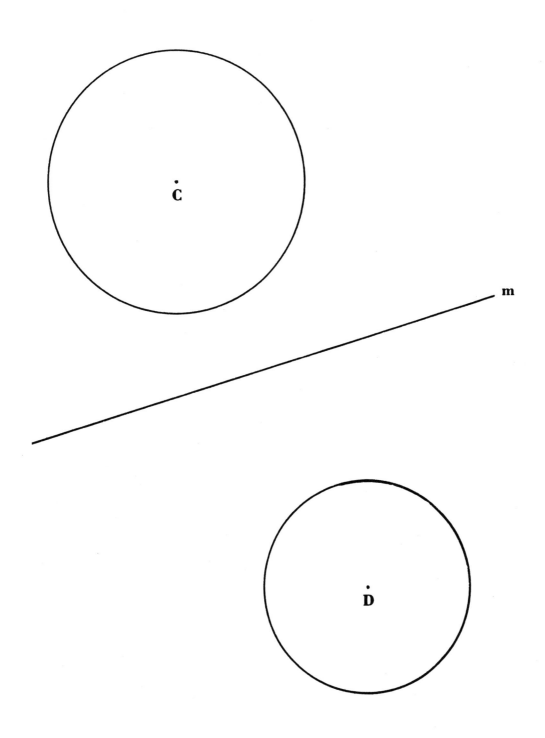

Find a line through P which intersects the two circles in chords of the same length.

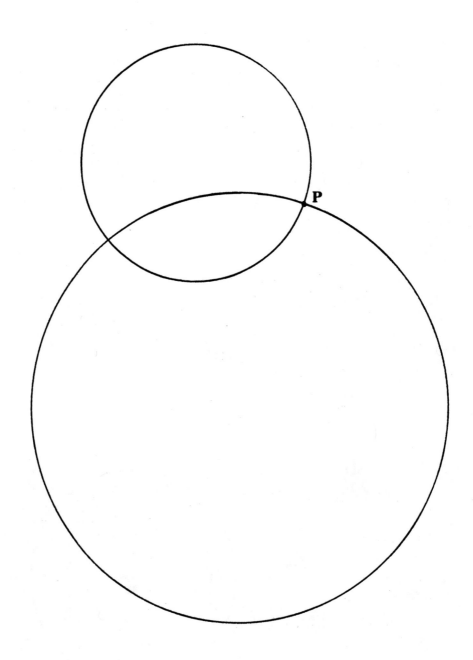

CHAPTER TWO

TRANSFORMATIONS

EXERCISE 2.1

Here are some figures. In each case figure 1 and figure 2 are translation images of each other.

Use tracing paper to verify that in each case figure 1 and figure 2 have the same size and same shape.

Trace figure 1 and then slide the tracing paper until the tracing coincides with figure 2.

△X′Y′Z′ is the image of △XYZ under a translation.

Compare:

(a) XX′, YY′, and ZZ′.

(b) XZ and X′Z′, XY and X′Y′, YZ and Y′Z′.

(c) m∠XYZ and m∠X′Y′Z′.

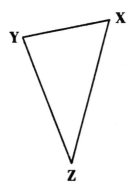

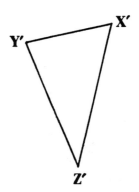

EXERCISE 2.3

T is the translation defined by T(A) = B and we say that B is the image of A under the translation T or that T maps A onto B.

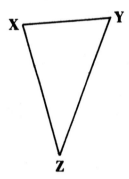

. **A**

. **B**

To find the image of △XYZ under the translation T:

1. Extend $\overrightarrow{AB}$.

2. Place tracing paper over this page. Trace the triangle and the points A and B.

3. Slide the tracing paper along $\overrightarrow{AB}$ so that the tracing paper A is on B and B is on $\overrightarrow{AB}$.

4. The position of the triangle on your tracing paper now corresponds to the position of the image of △XYZ under the translation T. If you press down hard with a sharp pencil, the image of the triangle can be seen on this page when you remove the tracing paper.

Can you locate T(B)?

EXERCISE 2.4

Try to guess where the image of each of these figures will be under the translation that
maps A onto A'.

Use the dots to help you draw the image figures.

Then verify your work with tracing paper.

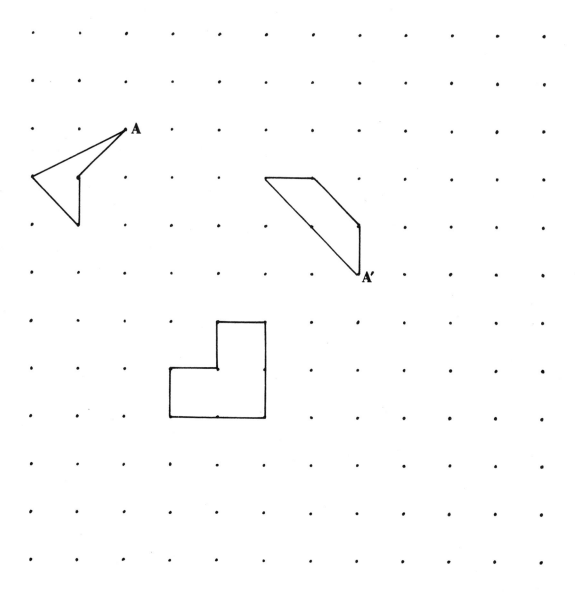

T is the translation defined by T(A) = A′.

Use tracing paper to locate B′ = T(B) and C′ = T(C).

Construct ⊙A′ with radius AB and ⊙B with radius AA′.

Describe the position of B′ relative to ⊙A′ and ⊙B.

Draw the line through A, C, and A′.

Construct ⊙C with radius AA′.

Describe the position of C′ relative to $\overleftrightarrow{AA′}$ and ⊙C.

Use your compass to locate T(D).

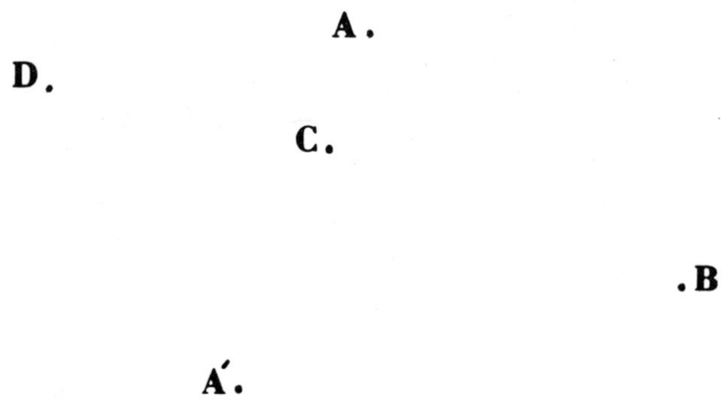

A.

D.

C.

.B

A′.

A transformation of the plane is a one-to-one function from the plane onto the plane.

A translation is a transformation since every point has exactly one image and every point

has exactly one preimage.

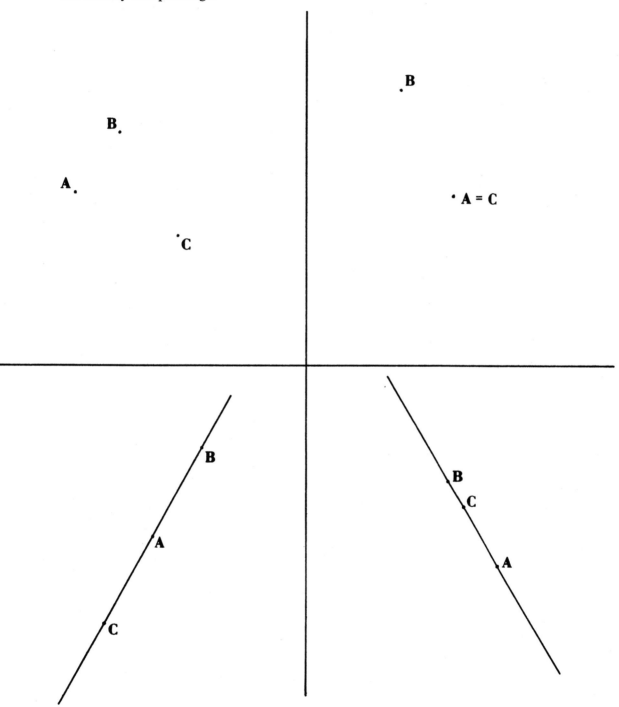

For each of the above, let T be the translation defined by T(A) = B.

Locate points X, Y, Z, and W so that T(B) = X, T(Y) = A, T(C) = Z, and T(W) = C.

EXERCISE 2.7

$\triangle A'B'C'$ is the image of $\triangle ABC$ under a translation.

Draw the perpendicular bisectors p of $\overline{AA'}$, m of $\overline{BB'}$ and q of $\overline{CC'}$.

What is true about p, m, and q?

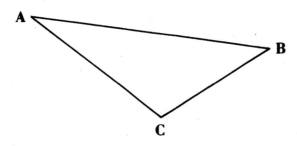

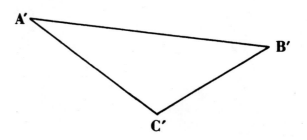

Let T and F be translations. Then the transformation "apply T, and then apply F to the images of T" is called the composite of F and T, denoted by F∘T.

This definition means: if P is a point, then F∘T(P) = F(T(P)).

T is the translation defined by T(A) = B and F is the translation defined by F(X) = Y.

To locate F∘T(P), locate P′ = T(P) and then locate P″ = F(P′).

Then P″ = F(P′) = F(T(P)) = F∘T(P).

Locate F∘T(Q) and T∘F(P).

A.

.Q

P.   .**B**

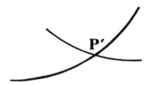

.**X**

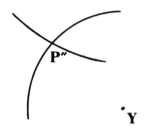

.**Y**

T is the translation defined by T(A) = A′, and F is the translation that maps B onto B′. Is T∘F(△XYZ) = F∘T(△XYZ)?

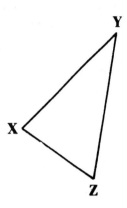

A′.

A.   **.B**

                              .B′

Locate:

    (a) △X′Y′Z′ = T(△XYZ)

    (b) △X″Y″Z″ = F(△XYZ)

    (c) F(△X′Y′Z′)

    (d) T(△X″Y″Z″).

EXERCISE 2.10

T is the translation defined by T(A) = A′, and F is the translation defined by F(B) = B′.

Show that T∘F is a translation G by identifying a point and its image under G.

Verify that T∘F = G by locating T(F(Q)) and G(Q).

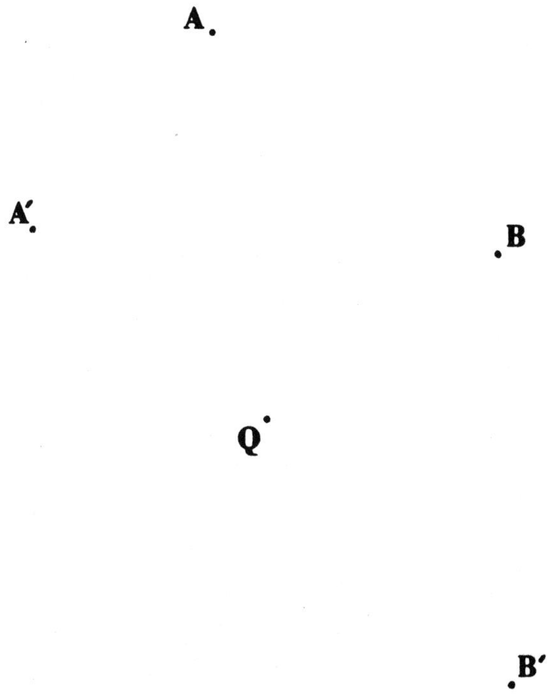

A.

A′.

.B

Q

.B′

EXERCISE 2.11

Here are some figures. In each case figure 1 and figure 2 are rotation images of each other.

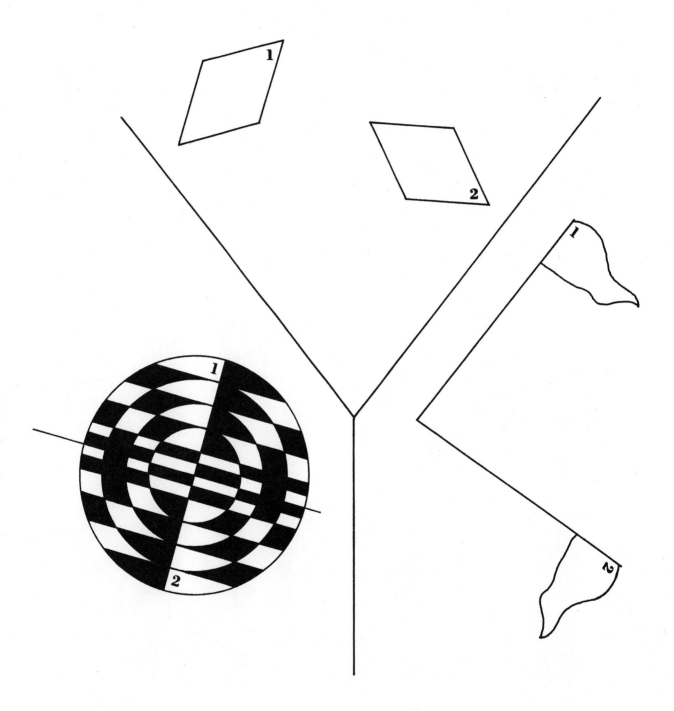

Use tracing paper to verify that in each case figure 1 and figure 2 have the same size and same shape.

Trace figure 1 and then rotate the tracing paper until the tracing coincides with figure 2.

△A′B′C′ is the image of △ABC under a rotation with center O.

Compare:

(a) AB and A′B′, AC and A′C′, BC and B′C′.

(b) m∠ABC and m∠A′B′C′, m∠BAC and m∠B′A′C′, m∠ACB and m∠A′C′B′.

Draw three concentric circles with center O, radii of OA, OB, and OC. Describe the
locations of A′, B′, and C′. What can you conclude about OA and OA′, OB and
OB′, OC and OC′?

Compare m∠AOA′, m∠BOB′, and m∠COC′.

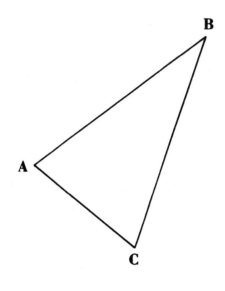
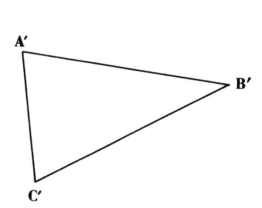

$\triangle A'B'C'$ is the image of $\triangle ABC$ under the rotation R with center O.

Draw the circles with center O, radii OA, OB, and OC.

Compare AA', BB', and CC'.

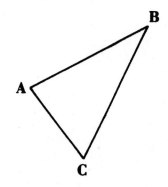

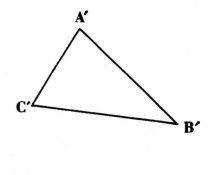

Ȯ

$\triangle X'Y'Z'$ is the image of $\triangle XYZ$ under a rotation with center C.

Construct the perpendicular bisectors p of $\overline{XX'}$, q of $\overline{YY'}$, and s of $\overline{ZZ'}$.

What is true about p, q, and s?

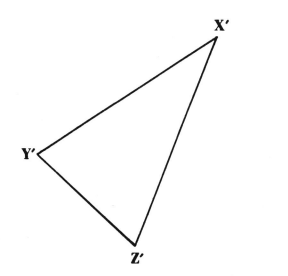

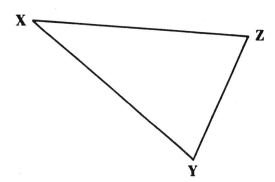

Y′ is the image of Y and X′ is the image of X under the rotation R.
Locate the center of the rotation R.

A rotation is a transformation of the plane. Every point has exactly one image and every

point has exactly one preimage.

EXERCISE 2.16

R is the rotation with center O. The measure of the angle of rotation is $a = m\angle XOY$. The direction of the rotation is clockwise.

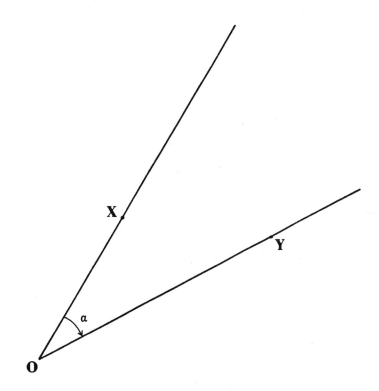

Find the image of R(P) of P.

1. Place tracing paper on this page.

2. Trace the points P and X.

3. With pencil held firmly on O, rotate the tracing paper until X is on $\overrightarrow{OY}$.

4. The position of P on your tracing paper now corresponds to the location of R(P) under the rotation R. If you press down hard with a sharp pencil, the image of P can be seen on this page when you remove the tracing paper.

Can you locate R(X), R(Y), and R(O)?

EXERCISE 2.17

R is the counterclockwise rotation with center C and the angle of rotation is β.

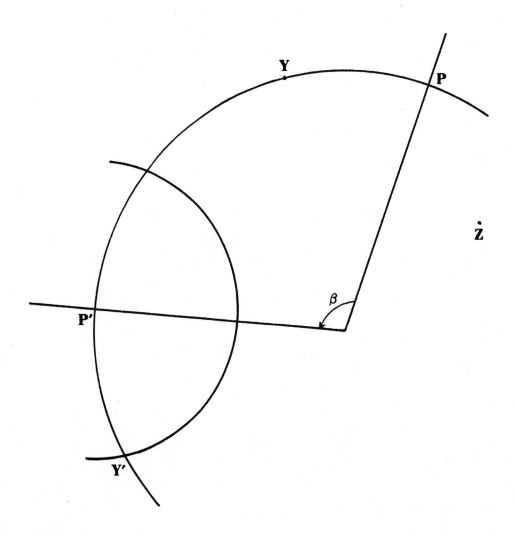

To locate $Y' = R(Y)$:

1. Draw $\odot C$ with radius CY and let P and P' be the points as indicated.

2. Draw $\odot P'$ with radius YP.

3. $\odot P'$ intersects $\odot C$ in two points. Y' is the one so that $m\angle YCY' = \beta$.

Locate $Z' = R(Z)$.

EXERCISE 2.18

In each of the following B is the image of A under a rotation R with center O.

Locate points X, Y, W, and V so that R(B) = X, R(Y) = A, R(C) = W, and R(V) = C.

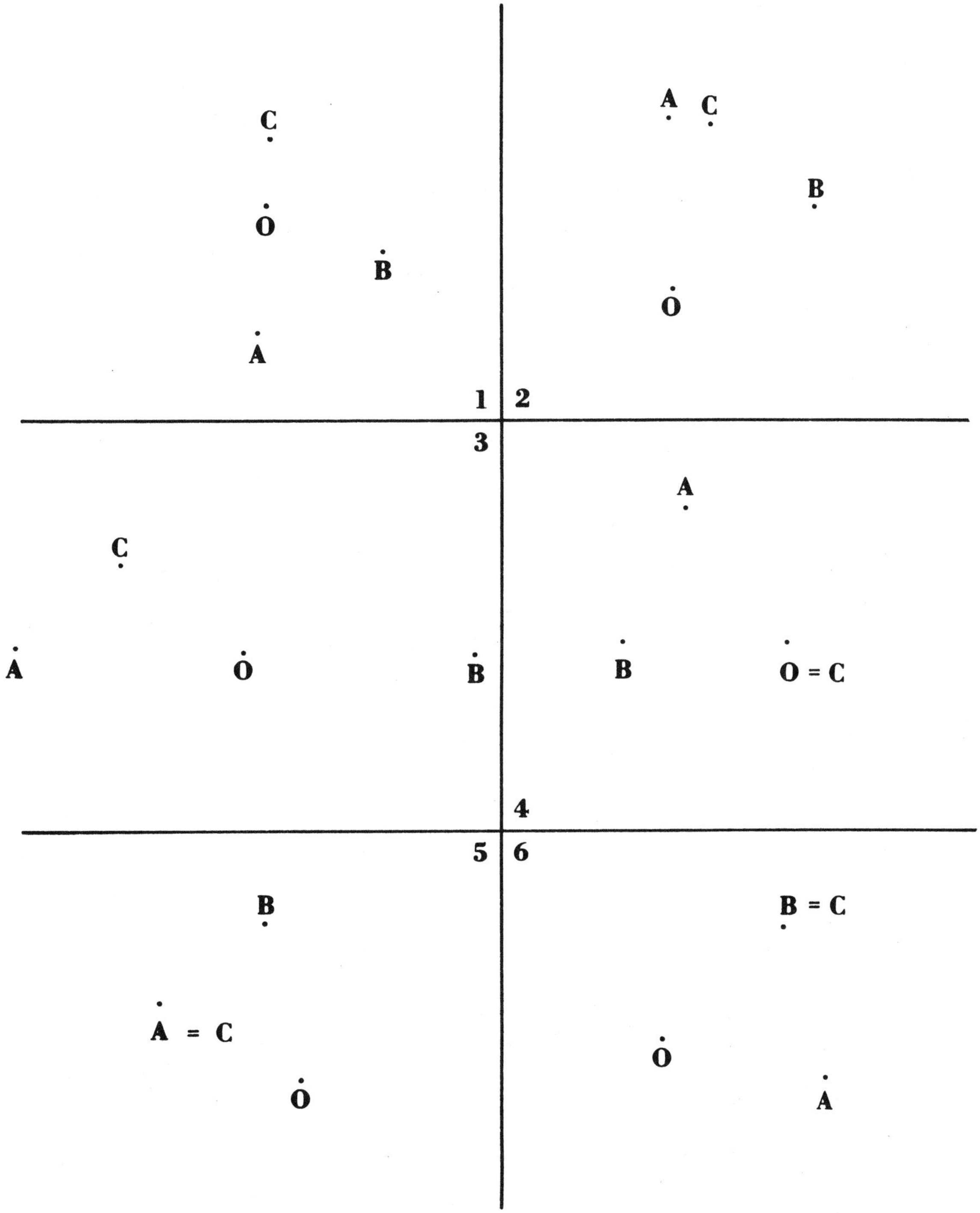

C
O
B
A

1   2

A   C
B
O

3

C
A   O   B

A
B   O = C

4

5   6

B
A = C
O

B = C
O
A

The rotation in (3) is called a half-turn, the measure of the angle of rotation being 180°.

In 1763, Sir John Bluebeard, the notorious pirate decided to bury a chest of gold on a small island in the Caribbean. The only markings that he used on his treasure map were the two palm trees and the wooden gallows as shown below. He paced the distance d_1 from the gallows to A, made a quarter turn in a counterclockwise direction and paced off the same distance d_1 to P. He returned to the gallows and paced off the distance d_2 to B, made a quarter turn in a clockwise direction and paced off d_2 to Q. He buried the treasure chest halfway between P and Q. Unfortunately he died without retrieving the treasure.

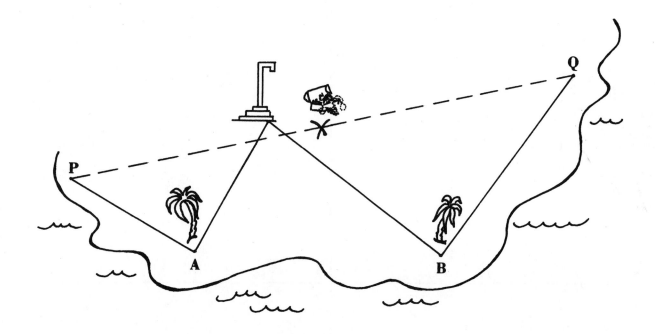

In 1977 the treasure map was found by the noted geometer, Pearl O. Graham, who immediately set sail for the island. She found the palm trees as marked, but the gallows had rotted away. This posed no problem for Pearl, who was a transformation geometry buff. She found the treasure immediately. Can you?

One morning young Michael started walking from his home to school. Being somewhat of a dreamer, he walked past the school. In fact he walked twice as far as he should have to S' (HS = SS'). Since he was late anyway, Michael decided to stroll through the park. Again he was daydreaming and walked twice as far as he should have to P' (S'P = PP'). Deciding to finish off the morning by going to the movie instead of school, our young friend did it again and wound up at M' (P'M = MM'). By this time the morning was gone, so he decided to make it to school for lunch. Repeating his earlier mistakes he stopped at S'', P'', and eventually ended his travels at M'' (M'S = SS'', S''P = PP'', and P''M = MM''). Can you describe where young Michael ended his trip?

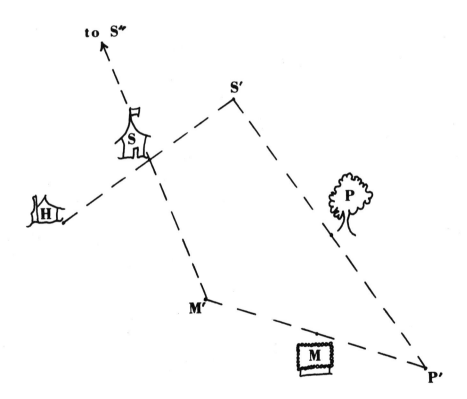

Let R_1 and R_2 be rotations. Then the transformation "apply R_1, and then apply R_2 to the images of R_1" is called the composite of R_2 and R_1, denoted by $R_2 \circ R_1$.

This definition means: if P is a point, then $R_2 \circ R_1 (P) = R_2 (R_1 (P))$.

R_a and R_β are clockwise rotations with center C. The measure of the angle of rotation for R_a is a and β for R_β.

To locate $R_a \circ R_\beta(P)$, locate $P' = R_\beta(P)$ and then locate $P'' = R_a(P')$.

Then $P'' = R_a(P') = R_a(R_\beta(P)) = R_a \circ R_\beta(P)$.

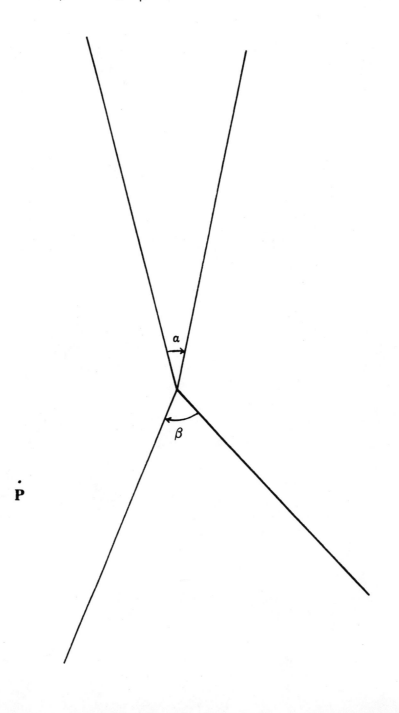

EXERCISE 2.22

R_a and R_β are clockwise rotations with center C. a is the measure of the angle of rotation for R and β is the measure of the angle of rotation for R.

Is $R_a \circ R_\beta(\triangle XYZ) = R_\beta \circ R_a(\triangle XYZ)$?

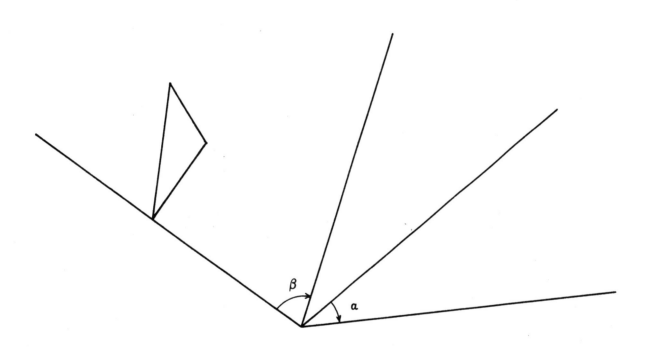

It may be easier to do this exercise with tracing paper than with a compass.

Locate:

  (a) $\triangle X'Y'Z' = R_a(\triangle XYZ)$.

  (b) $\triangle X''Y''Z'' = R_\beta(\triangle X'Y'Z')$.

  (c) $\triangle X'''Y'''Z''' = R_\beta(\triangle XYZ)$

  (d) $R_a(\triangle X''Y''Z'')$, which should coincide with $\triangle X'''Y'''Z'''$.

R_a and R_β are clockwise rotations with center C.

Show that $R_a \circ R_\beta$ is a rotation R by describing the center, the angle, and the direction
of the rotation.

Verify that $R_a \circ R_\beta = R$ by finding $R_a \circ R_\beta(Q)$ and R(Q).

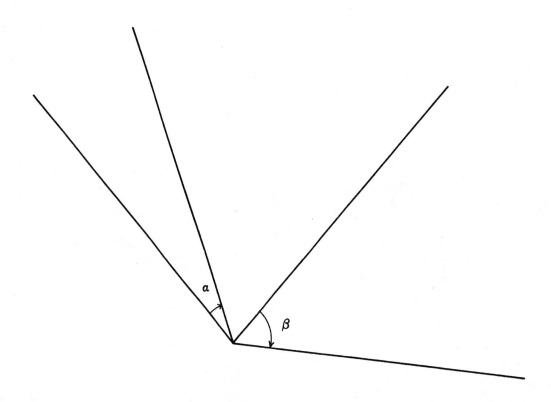

Here are some figures. In each case figure 1 and figure 2 are reflection images of each other.

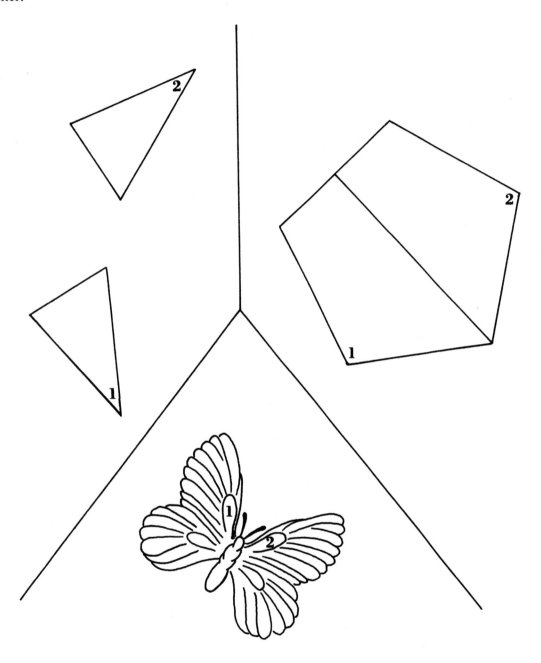

Use tracing paper to verify that in each case figure 1 and figure 2 have the same size and same shape. Trace figure 1 and then flip the tracing paper over to match the tracing with figure 2.

EXERCISE 2.25

Find the image of "P" under the reflection about line m.

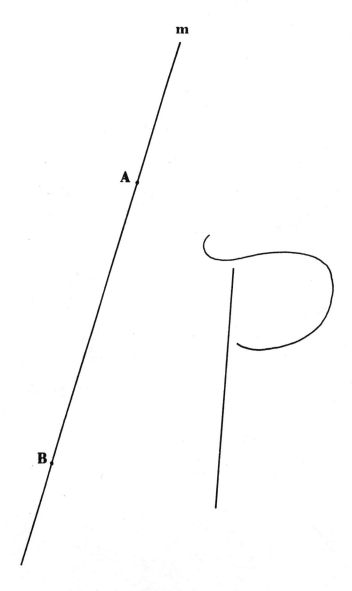

1. Cover this page with a sheet of tracing paper.

2. Draw the figure "P" and the points A and B on tracing paper.

3. Flip the tracing paper over and lay it down on this page so that the points A and B on the tracing paper coincide with the points A and B on this page.

4. The position of "P" on your tracing paper now corresponds to the position of the image of "P" under the reflection about line m. If you press down hard with a sharp pencil, the image of "P" can be seen on this page when you remove the tracing paper.

Triangles ABC and XYZ are reflection images of each other.

First construct the perpendicular bisectors of $\overline{AX}$, $\overline{BY}$, and $\overline{CZ}$.

Then while holding the paper towards a light, fold the paper so that the triangles coincide.

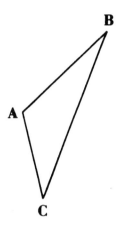

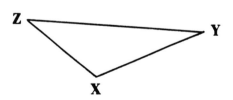

The perpendicular bisectors and the fold line should coincide.

This line is the reflection line.

EXERCISE 2.27

These figures are reflection images of each other. With your Mira locate the line p that reflects one figure onto the other.

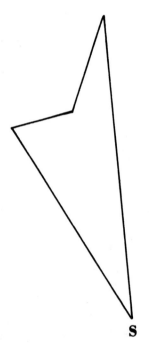

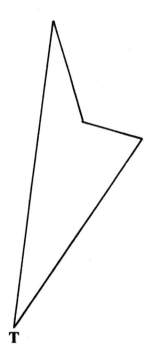

When you find the Mira line p that reflects one figure onto the other, S should coincide with the image of T.

Construct the perpendicular bisector of $\overline{ST}$. Do the Mira line and the perpendicular bisector coincide?

We say that T is the image of S under the reflection about p and write $r_p(S) = T$. Notice that it is also true that $r_p(T) = S$.

EXERCISE 2.28

Use your Mira to locate $r_m(A) = A'$, $r_m(B) = B'$, $r_m(C) = C'$, $r_m(D) = D'$, and $r_m(E) = E'$.

A, C, and E are collinear. What can you say about A', C', and E'?

Compare AB and $A'B'$, CE and $C'E'$.

Compare m∠DEC and m∠$D'E'C'$, m∠$CC'E$ and m∠$C'CE'$.

C is between A and E. How is C' related to A' and E'?

Compare AA' and CC'.

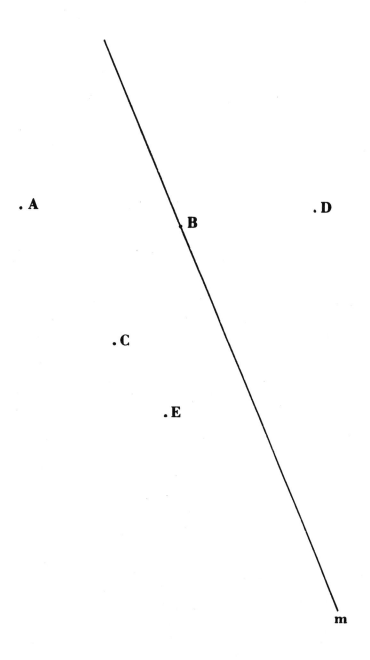

Locate $A' = r_m(A)$ and $B' = r_m(B)$.

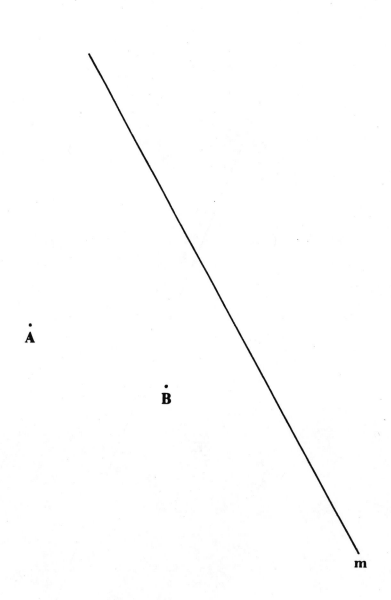

Where is the image X' of X if $X \in \overline{AB}$?

Where is the image Y' of Y if Y is any point on $\overleftrightarrow{AB}$?

Where is the image Z' of Z if Z is any point on $\overrightarrow{AB}$?

EXERCISE 2.30

$\overline{AC} \cap \overline{DE} = B$ and $\overline{AC} \cap m = F$.

What is true about $r_m(\overline{AC}) \cap r_m(\overline{DE})$? $r_m(\overline{AC}) \cap m$?

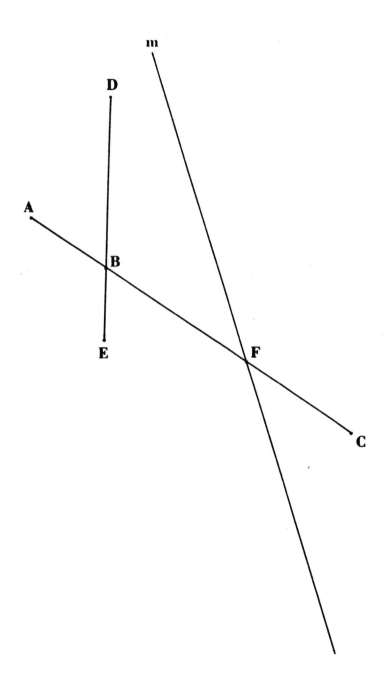

EXERCISE 2.31

Construct a triangle, a circle, and a quadrilateral so that each one is mapped onto itself under the reflection r_t.

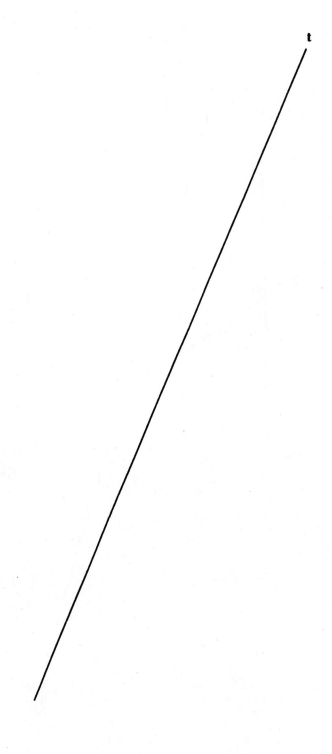

Let r_s and r_t be reflections. Then the transformation "apply r_s, and then apply r_t to the images of r_s" is called the composite of r_s and r_t, denoted by $r_t \circ r_s$.

This definition means: if P is a point, then $r_t \circ r_s(P) = r_t(r_s(P))$.

To locate $r_t \circ r_s(P)$, place the Mira on s and locate $P' = r_s(P)$.

Next place the Mira on t to locate $P'' = r_t(P')$.

Then $P'' = r_t \circ r_s(P)$.

Locate $r_t \circ r_s(Q)$ and $r_s \circ r_t(P)$.

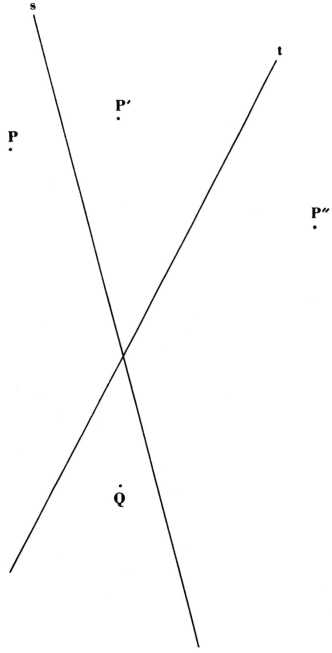

Note: A transformation is an isometry if and only if it is a reflection or a composite of reflections.

Determine if $r_p \circ r_q(X) = r_q \circ r_p(X)$ in each of the following.

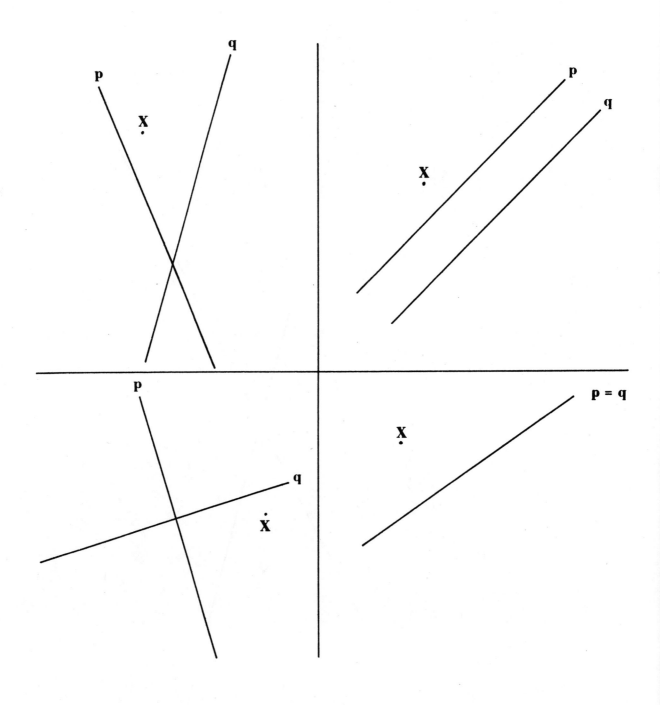

EXERCISE 2.34

$\triangle A'B'C'$ is the image of $\triangle ABC$ under the rotation R.

Note that $R(\triangle ABC) = \triangle A'B'C'$.

Locate the center O of the rotation and describe the angle of rotation.

Find two lines p and q so that $r_p \circ r_q(\triangle ABC) = R(\triangle ABC)$.

Compare the measure of the angle of rotation and the measure of the acute angle

     between p and q.

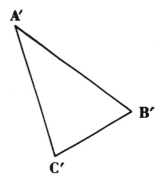

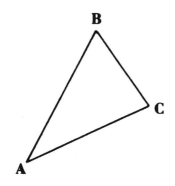

Locate $\triangle X'Y'Z' = r_p \circ r_q(\triangle XYZ)$.

Describe the rotation R that maps $\triangle XYZ$ onto $\triangle X'Y'Z'$.

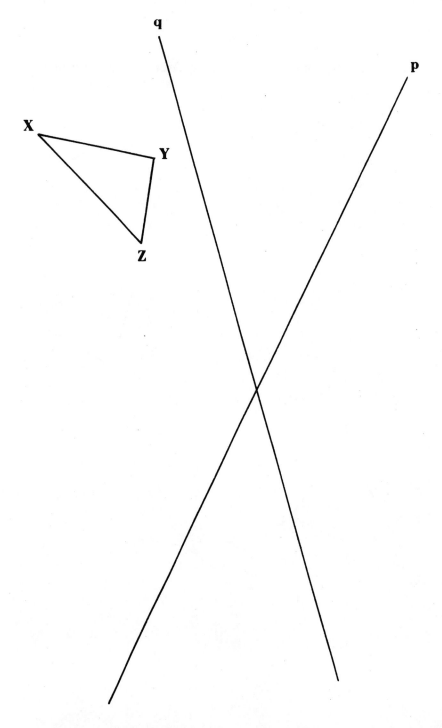

Note: This exercise demonstrates that if two distinct lines p and q are not parallel, then the isometry $r_p \circ r_q$ is a rotation.

In exercise 2.33 you found that $r_p \circ r_q = r_q \circ r_p$ if $p \perp q$.

The composite of two reflections about perpendicular lines is a half-turn.

To find the image $X' = r_p \circ r_q(X)$, draw the ray $\overrightarrow{XO}$ and with your Mira locate X' on $\overrightarrow{XO}$ so
    that $XO = OX'$.

Find $r_p \circ r_q(\triangle ABC)$.

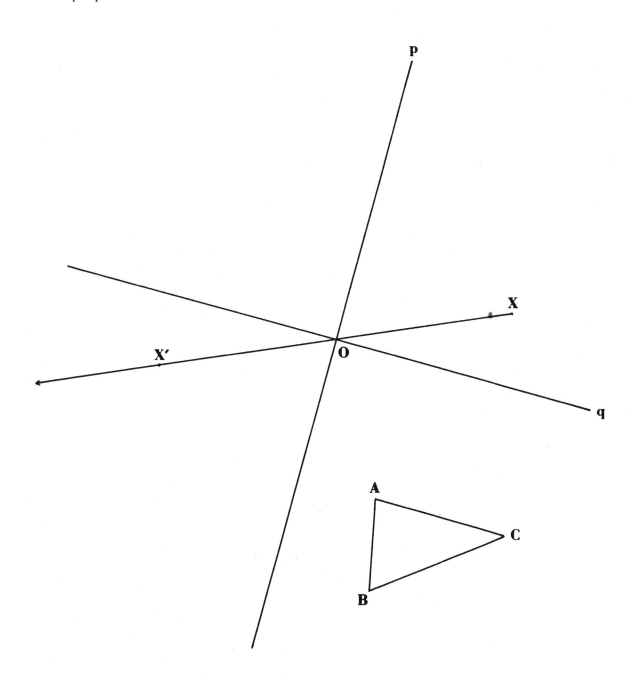

$\triangle P'Q'R'$ is the image of $\triangle PQR$ under the translation T.

Note that $T(\triangle PQR) = \triangle P'Q'R'$.

Locate two lines s and t so that $r_s \circ r_t(\triangle PQR) = T(\triangle PQR)$.

How are s and t related?

How are s and t related to the lines $\overleftrightarrow{PP'}$, $\overleftrightarrow{QQ'}$, and $\overleftrightarrow{RR'}$.

Compare the distance between s and t with PP', QQ', and RR'.

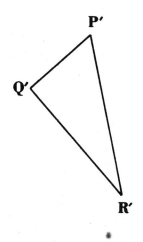

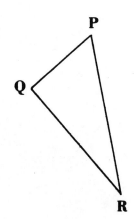

Locate $\triangle X'Y'Z' = r_m \circ r_n(\triangle XYZ)$.

Describe the translation T that maps $\triangle XYZ$ onto $\triangle X'Y'Z'$.

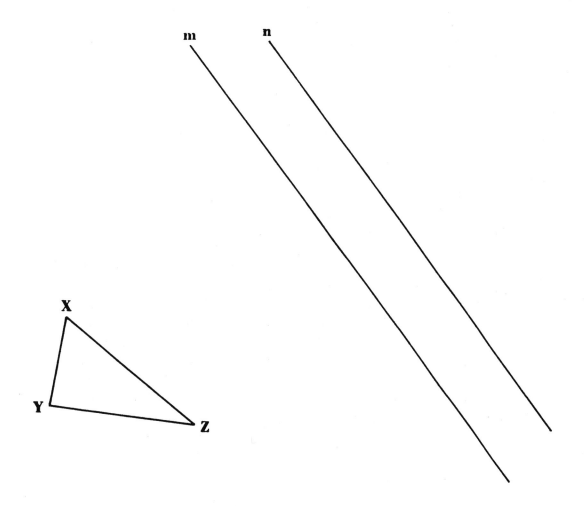

This exercise demonstrates that if two distinct lines m and n are parallel, then the isometry $r_m \circ r_n$ is a translation.

Find a line s so that $r_p \circ r_q \circ r_t(\triangle ABC) = r_s(\triangle ABC)$.

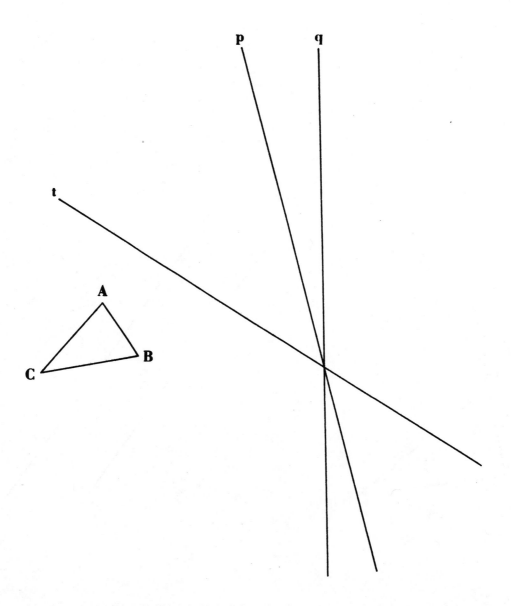

This exercise demonstrates that if three distinct lines t, q, and p are concurrent, then the isometry $r_p \circ r_q \circ r_t$ is a reflection.

Locate $r_s \circ r_t \circ r_p(\triangle ABC)$

Since t and p are parallel, what kind of isometry is $r_t \circ r_p$?

Notice that s is perpendicular to p and t.

Is $r_t \circ r_p \circ r_s = r_s \circ r_t \circ r_p$?

Locate the midpoints A'' of $\overline{AA'}$, B'' of $\overline{BB'}$, and C'' of $\overline{CC'}$.

Describe the location of A'', B'', and C''.

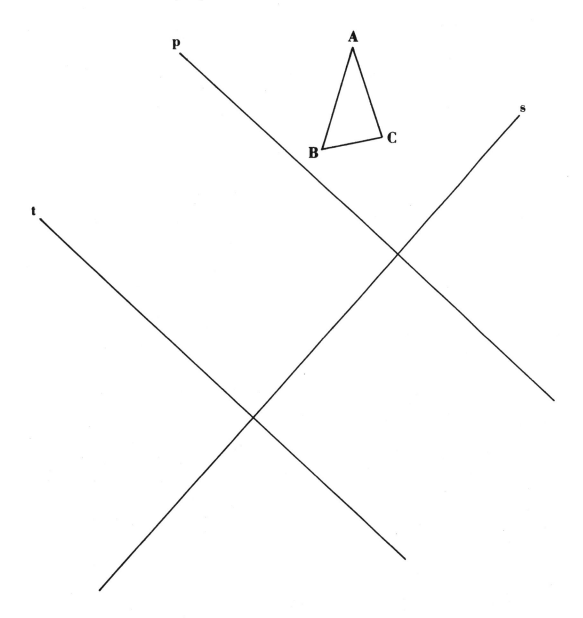

A glide reflection is the composite of a reflection r_s and a translation T with non-zero

magnitude and direction parallel to s.

EXERCISE 2.41

Find an isometry that maps △ABC onto △A'B'C'.

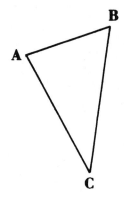

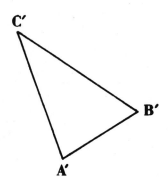

Draw the line s through the midpoints J of $\overline{AA'}$, K of $\overline{BB'}$, and L of $\overline{CC'}$.

Draw any line t so that t⊥s.

Locate $r_t \circ r_s(\triangle ABC)$

Then if p is the perpendicular bisector of $\overline{A'A''}$, then the isometry $r_p \circ r_t \circ r_s$ maps △ABC onto △A'B'C'.

Note: $r_p \circ r_t \circ r_s$ is a glide reflection.

Find a line m so that $r_t \circ r_p \circ r_s(\triangle XYZ) = r_m(\triangle XYZ)$.

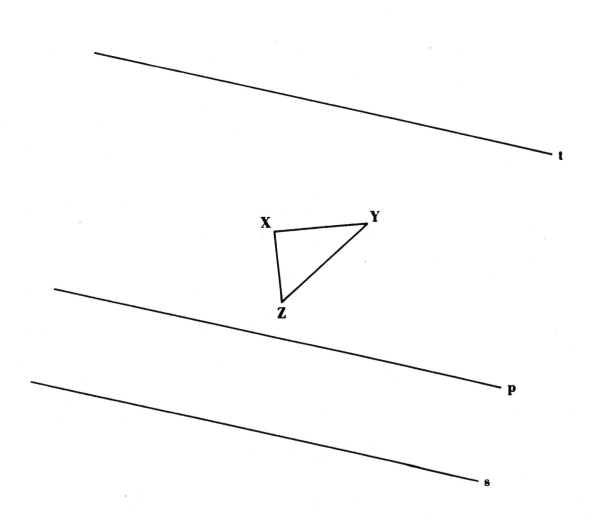

This exercise demonstrates that the composite of three reflections about lines that are parallel is a reflection.

Locate:

(a) $r_q \circ r_p \circ r_q(\triangle XYZ)$

(b) $r_p \circ r_q \circ r_p(\triangle XYZ)$

(c) $r_p \circ r_q \circ r_q(\triangle XYZ)$

(d) $r_q \circ r_q \circ r_p(\triangle XYZ)$

What can you conclude about $r_p \circ r_q \circ r_q$ and $r_q \circ r_q \circ r_p$?

Find lines m and n so that $r_m(\triangle XYZ) = r_q \circ r_p \circ r_q(\triangle AYZ)$ and $r_n(\triangle XYZ) = r_p \circ r_q \circ r_p(\triangle XYZ)$.

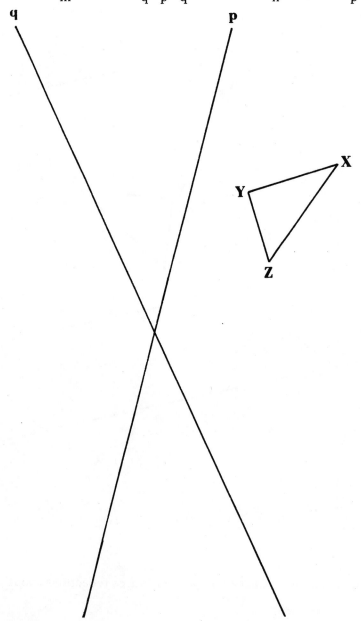

Compare the orientation of a triangle and the orientation of its image under one reflection,

the composite of two reflections, and the composite of three reflections.

EXERCISE 2.44

Let T be the translation defined by T(A) = B.

Locate $j' = T(j)$ and $k' = T(k)$.

Show that $r_k \circ r_j = r_{k'} \circ r_{j'}$ by finding the image of $\triangle DEF$ under each isometry.

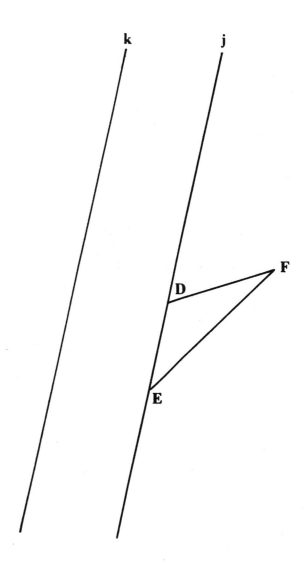

EXERCISE 2.45

Let R be the clockwise rotation with center C and angle of rotation with measure a.

Locate $p' = R(p)$ and $q' = R(q)$

Show that $r_p \circ r_q = r_{p'} \circ r_{q'}$ by finding the image of $\triangle HJK$ under each isometry.

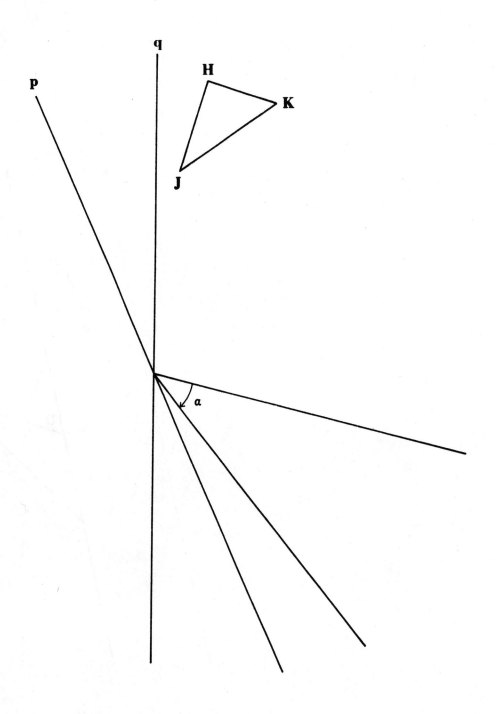

Find a rotation R that maps b onto c, and locate $a' = R(a)$.

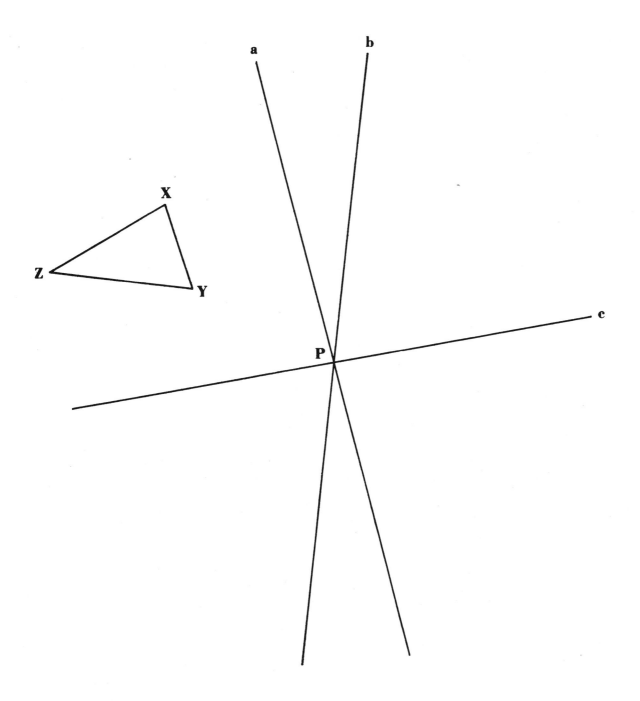

What can you conclude about the isometries $r_a \circ r_b$ and $r_{a'} \circ r_c$?

Show that $r_a \circ r_b \circ r_c = r_{a'}$ by finding the image of $\triangle XYZ$ under each isometry.

Find a translation T that maps p onto s, and locate $q' = T(q)$.

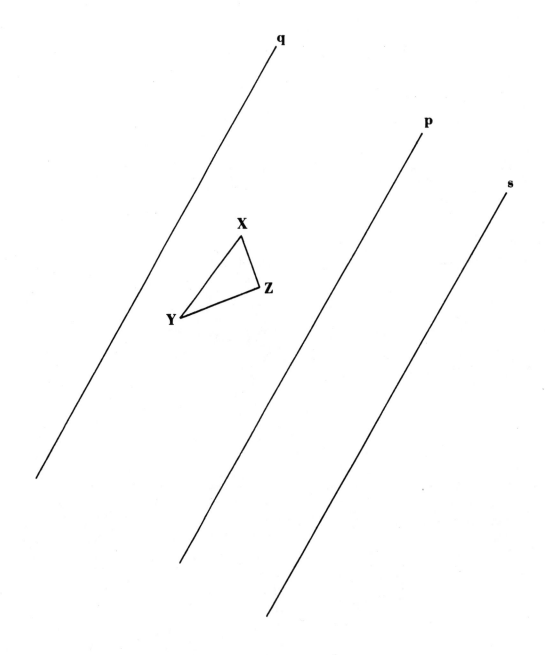

What can you conclude about the isometries $r_q \circ r_p$ and $r_{q'} \circ r_s$?

Show that $r_q \circ r_p \circ r_s = r_{q'}$ by finding the image of $\triangle XYZ$ under each isometry.

Find a rotation R so that if p′ = R(p), then p′⊥q.

Describe R by giving its center, direction, and rotation angle measure.

Find two lines so that R is the composite of reflections about these lines.

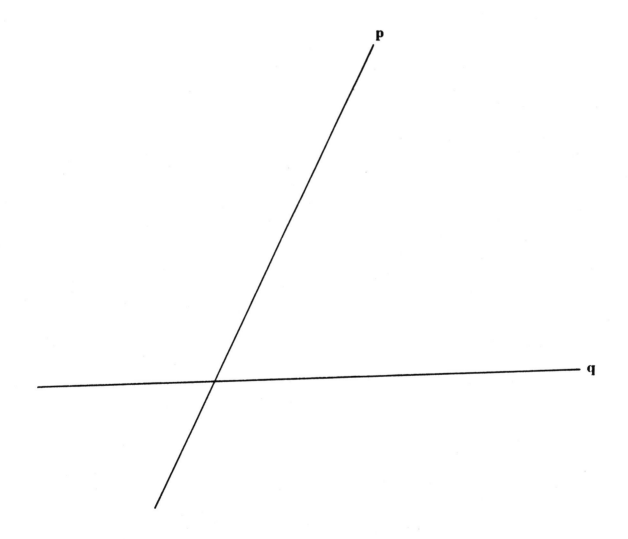

EXERCISE 2.49

Find the rotation R so that if $p' = R(p)$ and $s' = R(s)$, then $r_p \circ r_s = r_{p'} \circ r_{s'}$ and $s' \perp q$.

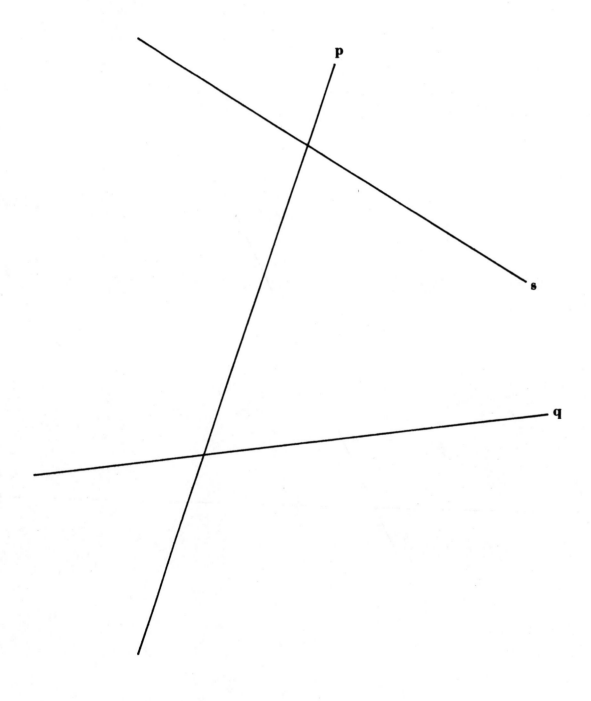

Find a rotation R so that if $t' = R(t)$ and $s' = R(s)$, then $s' \| p$ and $r_t \circ r_s = r_{t'} \circ r_{s'}$.

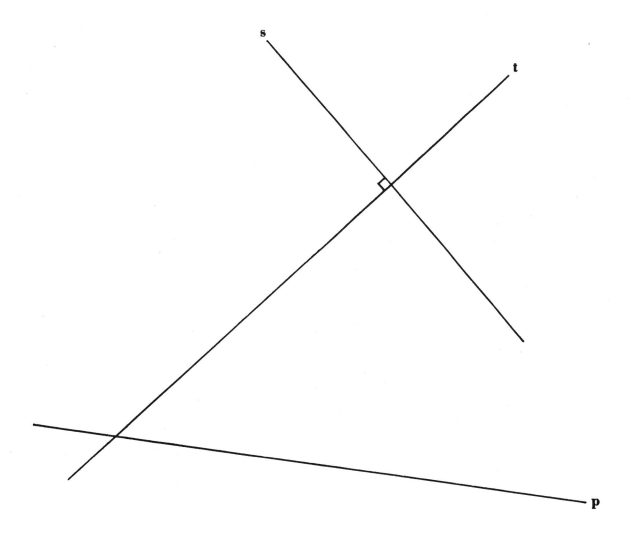

Note that s and t are perpendicular.

How are s' and t' related? How are t' and p related?

What kind of isometry is $r_{t'} \circ r_{s'} \circ r_p$?

EXERCISE 2.51

Find a rotation R_1 so that if $b' = R_1(b)$ and $a' = R(a)$, then $b' \perp c$ and $r_b \circ r_a = r_{b'} \circ r_{a'}$.
Draw a' and b', then find a rotation R_2 so that if $R_2(b') = b''$ and $R_2(c) = c'$, then

$r_c \circ r_{b'} = r_{c'} \circ r_{b''}$ and $b'' \parallel a'$.

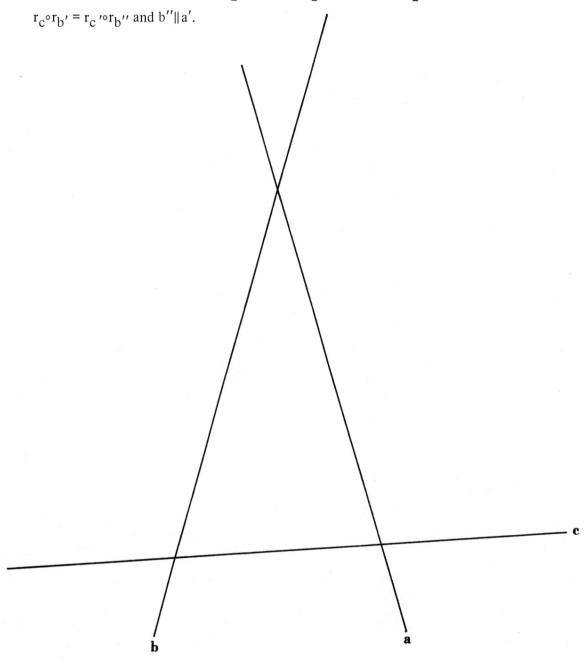

How are c' and a' related? How are c' and b'' related?

What kind of isometry is $r_{c'} \circ r_{b''} \circ r_{a'}$?

Show that $r_c \circ r_b \circ r_a = r_{c'} \circ r_{b''} \circ r_{a'}$.

Draw the line a so that $r_a(X) = X'$ and locate $r_a(Y)$ and $r_a(Z)$.

Draw the line b so that $r_b(r_a(Y)) = Y'$ and locate $r_b(r_a(Z))$.

Draw the line c so that $r_c(r_b(r_a(Z))) = Z'$.

Is $r_c \circ r_b \circ r_a(\triangle XYZ) = \triangle X'Y'Z'$?

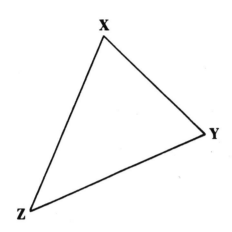

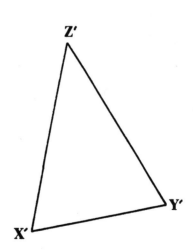

Note that $a \cap b \neq b \cap c$. What can you conclude about $r_c \circ r_b \circ r_a$?

Compare this exercise with exercise 2.51.

Let S be an isometry such that S(P) = P.

Let A and B be any two distinct points with A≠P≠B.

Remember that an isometry preserves distance since any isometry is a reflection or a composite of reflections.

So if S(A) = A′, then PA = PA′. That is, A′ ∈ ⊙P with radius PA.

Describe the possible locations for S(B) and describe the type of isometry S would be in each case.

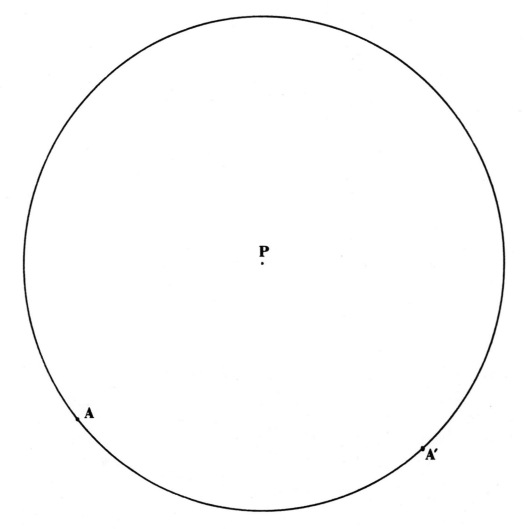

Let M be an isometry such that for any point P, M(P)≠P. That is, if M(P) = P′, then

P≠P′.

Let A be any point and let M(A) = A′.

Let p be the perpendicular bisector of $\overline{AA'}$.

What is the image of A under the isometry $r_p \circ M$?

Compare $r_p \circ M$ with S of the previous exercise.

Since $r_p \circ r_p = I$, the identity transformation, $r_p \circ r_p \circ M = M$.

Can you describe the type of isometry M is?

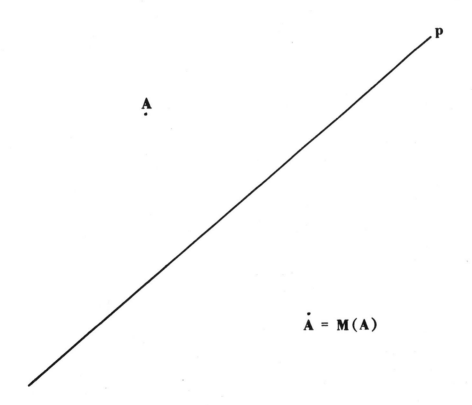

This exercise and the previous exercise shows that any isometry is the composite of at

most three reflections.

Rotations and translations are the only composites of two reflections. The composite

of three reflections is either a reflection or a glide reflection.

Thus there are exactly four types of isometries: reflections, rotations, translations,

and glide reflections.

EXERCISE 2.55

Here are some figures. In each case figure 1 and figure 2 are size transformation images of each other.

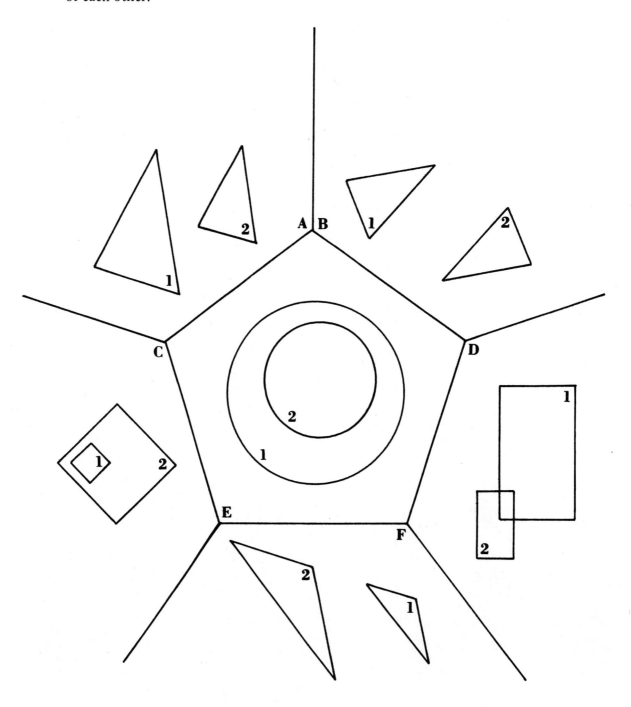

Which of these size transformations is also an isometry?

EXERCISE 2.56

△A′B′C′ is the image of △ABC under a size transformation.

Draw $\overleftrightarrow{AA'}$, $\overleftrightarrow{BB'}$, and $\overleftrightarrow{CC'}$.

Compare: (a) AB and A′B′

(b) AA′and BB′

(c) m∠ABC and m∠A′B′C′

(d) $\dfrac{AB}{A'B'}$ and $\dfrac{BC}{B'C'}$.

How are $\overleftrightarrow{AB}$ and $\overleftrightarrow{A'B'}$ related?

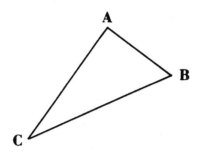

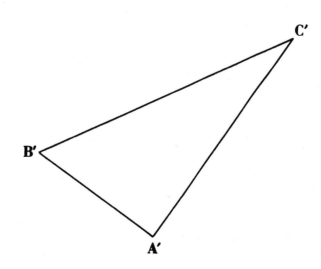

Let $D_{C, P, Q}$ denote the size transformation with center C that maps P to Q.

To find X′ the image of X:

    1. Draw $\overleftrightarrow{CP}$, $\overleftrightarrow{CX}$, and $\overline{PX}$.

    2. Through Q construct the line m parallel to $\overline{PX}$.

Then X ′= m ∩ CX = $D_{C,P,Q}$ (X)

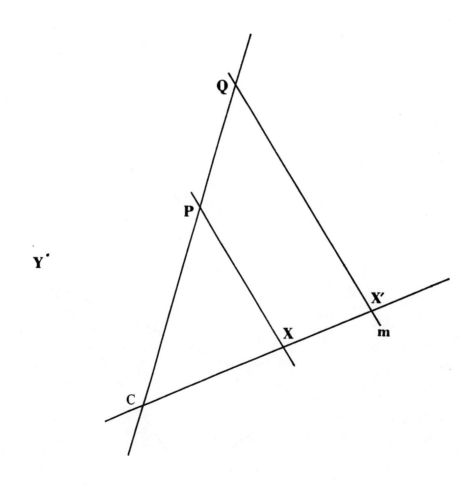

Locate $D_{C,P,Q}(Y)$.

$D_{C,P,Q}$ is the size transformation with center C that maps P to Q.

To find X′ the image of X where $X \in \overleftrightarrow{PQ}$:

1. Choose any point R so that $R \notin \overleftrightarrow{PQ}$.

2. Draw $\overleftrightarrow{CR}$.

3. Find the image R′ of R under $D_{C,P,Q}$ as in Exercise 2.55.

4. Similarly find $D_{C,R,R'}$ (X).

$X' = D_{C,R,R'} (X) = D_{C,P,Q} (X)$.

Locate $D_{C,P,Q}(Y)$.

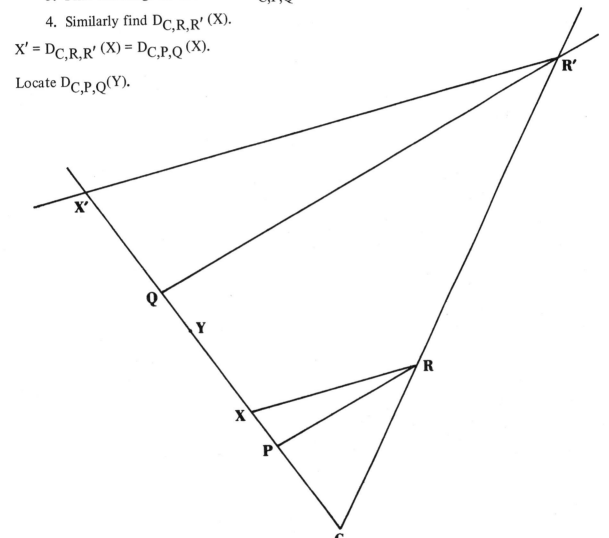

Locate $D_{C,P,Q} (Y)$.

EXERCISE 2.59

Locate $D_{C,P,Q}(S)$ and $D_{C,P,Q}(T)$.

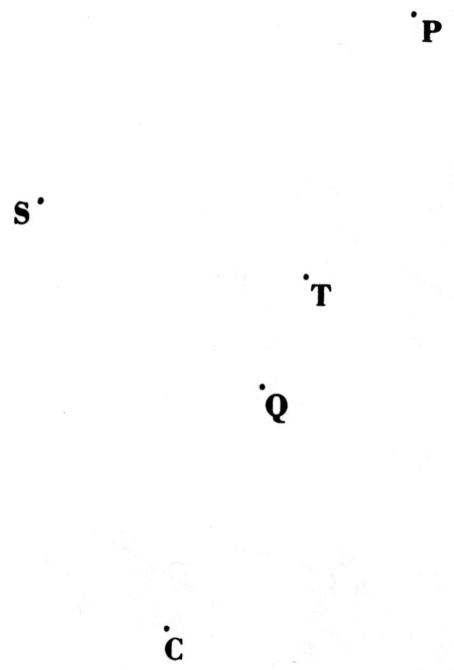

. P

S .

. T

. Q

. C

Locate $D_{C,P,Q}$ (J) and $D_{C,P,Q}$ (K).

$\dot{P}$

$\dot{C}$ $\dot{J}$

$\dot{Q}$

$\dot{K}$

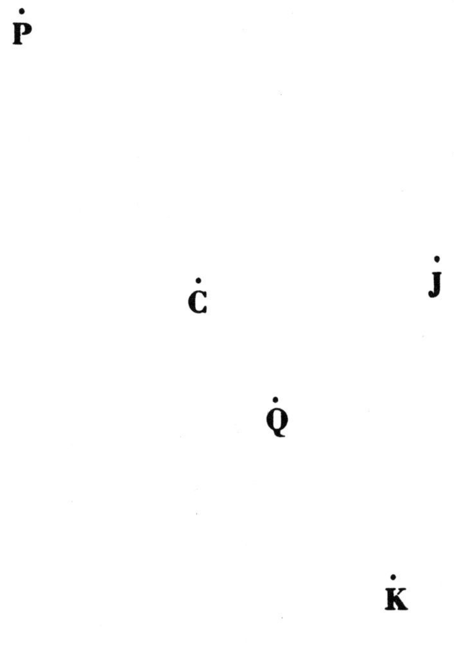

In each of the following Q is the image of P under a size transformation D. Locate C the center of the size transformation.

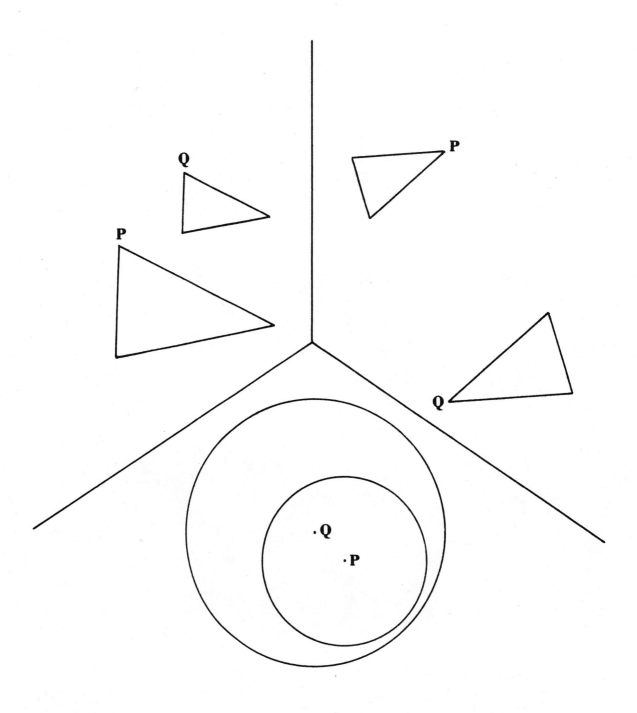

Find a transformation that is a composite of an isometry and a size transformation that
maps △ABC onto △A'B'C'.

To find S the isometry, locate a composite of reflections that maps an angle of △ABC
onto its corresponding angle of △A'B'C', say ∠BAC to ∠B'A'C', so that if Y is the
image of B and X is the image of C, then Y ∈ $\overline{A'B'}$ and X ∈ $\overline{A'C'}$.

Then find D a size transformation that maps △A'YX onto △A'B'C'.

D∘S(△ABC) = △A'B'C'.

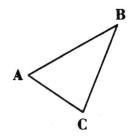

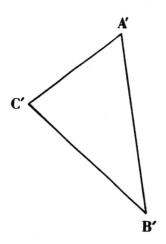

If a geometric figure can be mapped onto another geometric figure under the composite

of an isometry and a size transformation, then we say that the two figures are similar.

The composite of an isometry and a size transformation is called a similarity transformation.

Show that ΔJKL and ΔFGH are similar by describing a similarity transformation that maps

one onto the other.

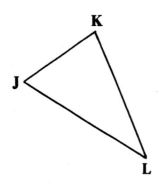

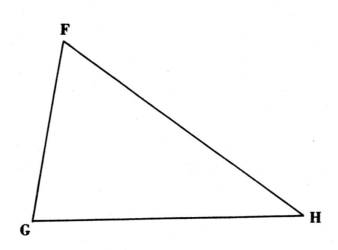

SOLUTIONS

To

Selected Exercises

A dotted line in a figure indicates a Mira line used to complete a construction.

1.3 Use the edge of the stream as a Mira line and locate the image B′ of B. Then $\overline{HB'}$ intersects the stream at the point P so that HP + PB is the shortest possible.

1.4 $\overleftrightarrow{AA'}$ and m are perpendicular; $\overleftrightarrow{AA'}$ and s are parallel.

1.5 Place the Mira on A in such a way that the image of s is s.

1.7 Place the Mira across $\overline{AB}$ so that the image of A is B.

1.8 Using m as a Mira line, let A be a point of intersection of ⊙C and the image of ⊙D. The construction may be impossible or there may be one or two solutions.

1.9 Place the Mira on Y so that $\overrightarrow{YZ}$ is reflected onto $\overrightarrow{YX}$.

1.11 Place the Mira between lines p and m so that p is the image of m.

1.13 (a) Using the midline of $\overleftrightarrow{AB}$ and p as a Mira line, the images of A and B will be the required points A′ and B′.

(b) To locate E, use a Mira line that contains C to reflect D onto p. Then E is the image of D.

(c) Use the perpendicular bisector of $\overline{AY}$ as a Mira line to locate B″ the image of B. Then as in (b), find a point X on p so that YB″ = XY. AB = XY″ and YB″ = YX, so AB = YX.

1.15 Place the Mira perpendicular to s so that the Mira is not on A. Locate the Mira image A′ of A. Then $\overleftrightarrow{AA}$ is parallel to S.

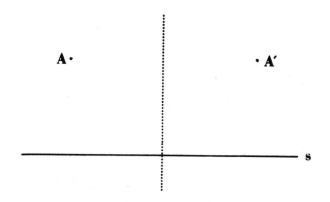

1.17 Use the line through P parallel to q as a Mira line to locate the image q′ of q. Then
q′ ∩ ⊙O gives the required endpoint(s) in ⊙O.

1.18 AB = A′B′ = A″B′ = XY.

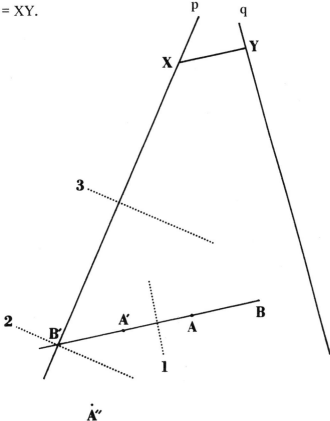

1.21 As in Exercise 1.8, locate points A and D so that q is the perpendicular bisector
of $\overline{AD}$. Then $\overline{AD}$ is a diagonal of the required square.

1.23 The Mira line through the midpoint of $\overline{PQ}$ reflects Q onto the perpendicular
bisector of $\overline{PQ}$. R is the image of Q.

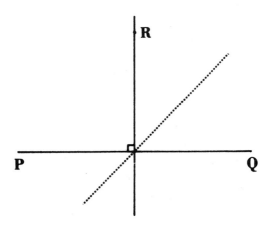

1.24 Locate a point C so that m∠CBA is 135° and CB = BA. Note that a 135° angle is the supplement of a 45°angle, so the construction is similar to Exercise 1.10.

1.25 Use perpendicular lines and remember the Pythagorean Theorem.

1.26 AB = BC = CD = DE = EF = 1

AC = $\sqrt{2}$

AD = $\sqrt{3}$

AE = $\sqrt{4}$

AF = $\sqrt{5}$

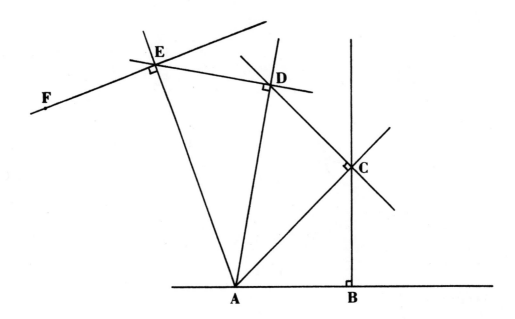

1.27 AZ = ZY = YW = WV = VU. Lines through Z, Y, W, and V are parallel to $\overrightarrow{UB}$.

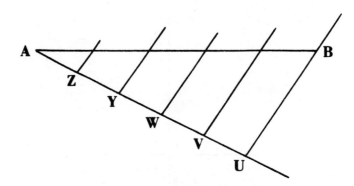

1.28   CR = a, RD = b, and line p is perpendicular to $\overline{CD}$ at R. The Mira line through the midpoint M of $\overline{CD}$ reflects C onto S.

SR = x.

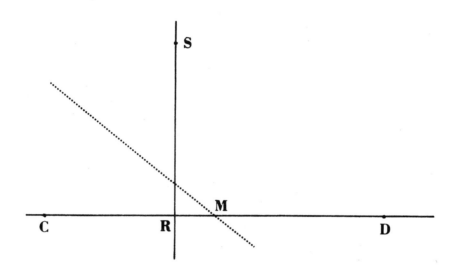

1.32   The point common to the three bisectors of the interior angles of a triangle is called the incenter of the triangle.

1.33   The incenter of the triangle is the center of the inscribed circle. A perpendicular from the incenter to one side of the triangle gives the radius of the inscribed circle.

1.35   The bisectors of two exterior angles and the bisector of the third interior angle are concurrent. These three points are called the excenters of the triangle. Each side of the triangle will be tangent to an excircle.

1.41   Through any vertex, say B, draw a line g parallel to m. Let K denote the point of
       intersection of the line g and the circumcircle.

       Through K, draw a line h perpendicular to the side $\overleftrightarrow{AC}$ opposite B. Let M = h ∩ $\overline{AC}$
       and let P denote the point of intersection of the line p and the circumcircle. Then
       P is the required point.

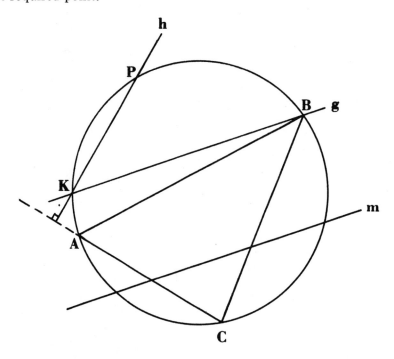

1.42   The point at which the medians are concurrent is called the centroid of the triangle.
       The centroid has the property that it divides each median of the triangle in the
       ratio 2/1.

1.45   The mira line through B reflects A onto the perpendicular bisector of $\overline{AB}$. C is
       the image of A.

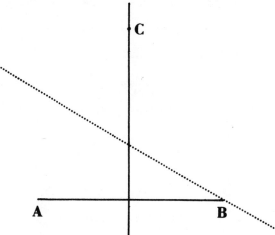

       Note: The Mira line makes a 30° angle with $\overrightarrow{BA}$.

146

1.46   Choose any point P on the circle.

Draw the two Mira lines through P that reflect the center of the circle onto the circle.

The equilateral triangle is determined by the points of the intersection of the Mira lines and the circle.

1.48   Let 0 be the center of the circles.

Choose a point P on the middle circle.

Locate a point S so that m∠SPO = 30° as in Exercise 1.45.

Use $\overleftrightarrow{PS}$ as a Mira line to locate the points Q and Q' of intersection of the image of the small circle with the large circle.

Let the perpendicular bisector of $\overline{PQ}$ intersect the small circle in R, and the perpendicular bisector of $\overline{PQ'}$ intersect the small circle in R'.

Then △PQR and △PQ'R' are equilateral.

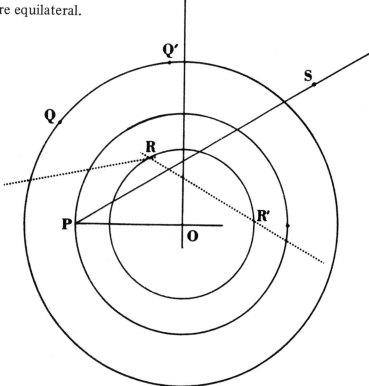

1.49   In a 30-60-90 triangle the hypotenuse has length twice the length of the leg opposite the 30° angle.

1.50   Draw a line h perpendicular to $\overline{KL}$ at L.

Extend $\overrightarrow{KL}$ and locate the point K' on $\overrightarrow{KL}$ so that KL = LK'.

Now find m the Mira line through K that reflects K' onto h.

Then J = h ∩ m.

Note: If K'' is the image of K' under the reflection about m, then KK'K'' is an equilateral triangle and m bisects a 60° angle.

147

1.52   Q′ is the image of Q over Mira line c, and d is the Mira line through Q′ that reflects Q onto c. P = d ∩ a. If f is the perpendicular bisector of $\overline{PQ}$, f ∩ c = R.

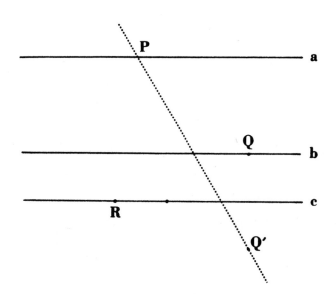

1.53   Given: OP = PS, n∥$\overline{OY}$, m⊥$\overline{OY}$, n ∩ m = P.

   The Mira line b reflects S onto T and reflects O onto R. T is on m and R is on n.
Proof that $m\angle O_2 = 2(m\angle O_1)$:
Let $\overline{OR}$ ∩ m = Q. T is the reflection image of S and R is the reflection image of O, so $m\angle O_2 = m\angle R_{1\,2}$ since reflections preserve angle measure.
$\overline{ST}$ and $\overline{OR}$ are parallel, since the reflecting line b is the perpendicular bisector of $\overline{ST}$ and $\overline{OR}$. $\angle O_2 \cong \angle S_1$ since they are alternate interior angles of parallel lines.
$\angle P_1$ and $\angle P_4$ are vertical angles, so they are congruent.
Then $\triangle OPQ \cong \triangle SPT$ by ASA.
$\overline{QP} \cong \overline{TP}$ since corresponding parts of congruent figures are congruent.
Since m⊥n, $\angle P_{3\,4} \cong \angle P_2$.
Then $\triangle TPR \cong \triangle QPR$ by SAS, and $\angle R_1 \cong \angle R_2$ since they are corresponding parts of congruent triangles.
$\angle O_1$ and $\angle R_2$ are alternate interior angles of the parallel lines, n and $\overleftrightarrow{OY}$ and so they have the same measure.
$m\angle O_1 = m\angle R_2$ and $m\angle O_2 = m\angle R_{1\,2} = m\angle R_1 + m\angle R_2 = 2(m\angle R_2)$, so $m\angle O_2 = 2(m\angle O_1)$.

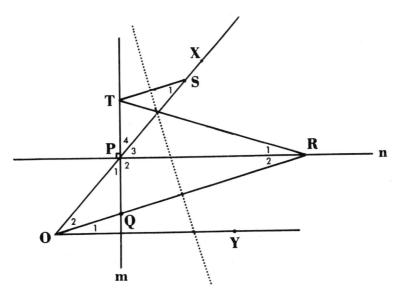

1.54 The idea for this construction involving a compass is due to Archimedes (ca.287-212 B.C.).

Given: The Mira line m reflects S onto S′ and reflects Q onto Q′. S′ is on $\overrightarrow{QP}$ and Q′ is on $\overset{\frown}{PR}$.

Proof that m∠RQQ′ = 2(m∠Q′QP):

m∠S′QQ′ = m∠SQ′Q since reflections preserve angle measure.

△SQQ′ is isosceles since $\overline{SQ}$ and $\overline{QQ′}$ are radii of ⊙Q, so m∠SQ′Q = m∠Q′SQ.

m∠Q′QR = 2(m∠Q′SR) since the measure of an inscribed angle is one-half the measure of its related central angle.

Hence, m∠Q′QR = 2(m∠Q′QP)

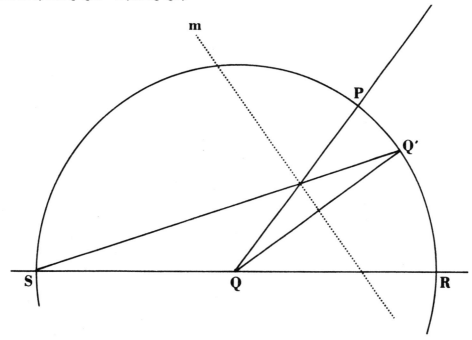

1.56   Each of the nine congruent arcs would contain 40° = 30° + 1/3(30°), or alternately 40° = 1/3(120°).

1.57   Line m is the perpendicular bisector of $\overline{AB}$. Using the first Mira line, P is the image of A on m. Then m∠ABP = 60° and its supplement measures 120°. QP = PB, and p is perpendicular to m at P. The second Mira line reflects Q onto Q′ and B onto B′. Then m∠QBB′ = 80 = 2/3(120).

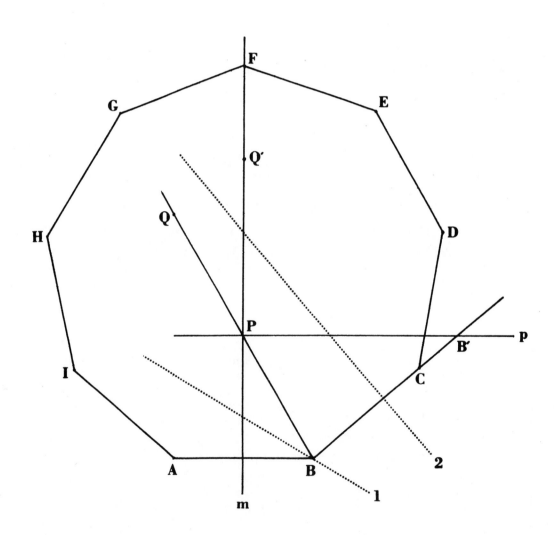

1.58   Draw m the perpendicular bisector of $\overline{AB}$.

Find a Mira line that reflects A onto m and B onto ⊙B.

Then C is the image of B, and D is the image of A.

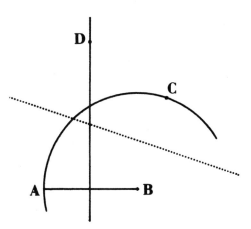

1.61   Mira lines that reflect the circle onto itself contain the center of the circle

1.65   Draw the Mira line m through A that reflects the circle onto itself.

Then the Mira line through A that reflects m onto itself is the tangent t.

1.66   The tangency point is O′ the image of O in a Mira line through the midpoint M of $\overline{OB}$.

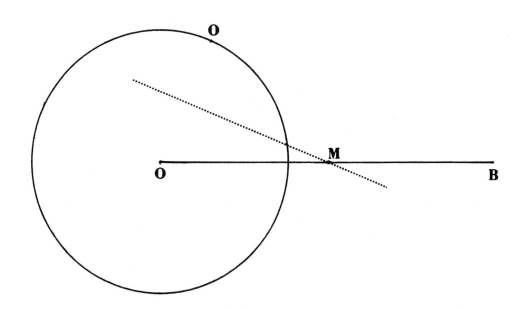

1.67   Draw a ray $\overrightarrow{AS}$.

Locate points P, Q, and R on $\overline{AS}$ so that AP = x, PQ = y, and AR = y.

Draw the line through Q and B, and draw a line p through P so that p‖$\overline{QB}$. Then if D = p ∩ $\overrightarrow{AB}$, x/y = AD/DB

Draw the line through R and B, and draw the line r through P parallel to $\overline{RB}$. Then if E = r ∩ $\overrightarrow{AB}$, x/y = AE/AB.

Draw the line through P and B, and draw the line m through R parallel to $\overline{PB}$. Then if F = m ∩ $\overrightarrow{AB}$, x/y = AB/AF.

Draw the line n through Q so that n‖$\overline{PB}$. Then if G = n ∩ $\overrightarrow{AB}$, x/y = AB/BG.

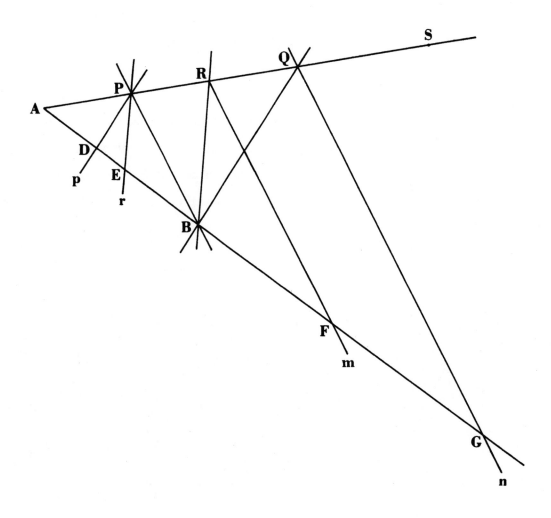

1.72   Let P be any point on ⊙D.

Locate the point Q on $\overrightarrow{CA}$ so that AW = DP and so that A is between C and Q.

Then ⊙Q with radius QA is the required circle.

152

1.73   Extend a radius, say $\overrightarrow{AS}$, of $\odot$A. Locate the point C' on $\overrightarrow{AS}$ so that SC' = radius

$\odot$C and so that S is between A and C'.

Locate P $\in \overline{AS}$ and Q $\in \overline{SC'}$ so that PS = SQ = radius of $\odot$B.

Locate the point M on $\overline{PQ}$ so that $\dfrac{PM}{MQ} = \dfrac{\text{radius } \odot A}{\text{radius } \odot C}$

(PY = radius $\odot$A and YZ = radius $\odot$C).

Draw a line m perpendicular to $\overline{AC'}$ at M. Then B' is the point on m so that

C'B' = PC' = radius $\odot$C + radius $\odot$B.

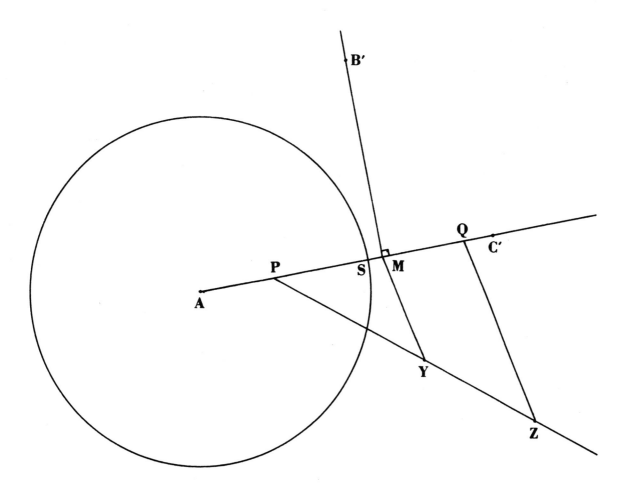

1.75   Draw the tangent t to $\odot$C at P.

Let $\odot$C' be the image of $\odot$C in the Mira line t.

Locate X = $\odot$C' $\cap$ $\odot$D, X $\neq$ P.

Let $\overrightarrow{XP}$ intersect $\odot$C at Y $\neq$ P.

Then $\overline{XP}$ is a chord of $\odot$D and $\overline{PY}$ is a chord of $\odot$C with XP = PY.

2.2 Exercise (a) demonstrates that the distance between a point and its image is constant under a translation.

Exercises (b) and (c) demonstrate that distance and angle measure are preserved under a translation.

2.3

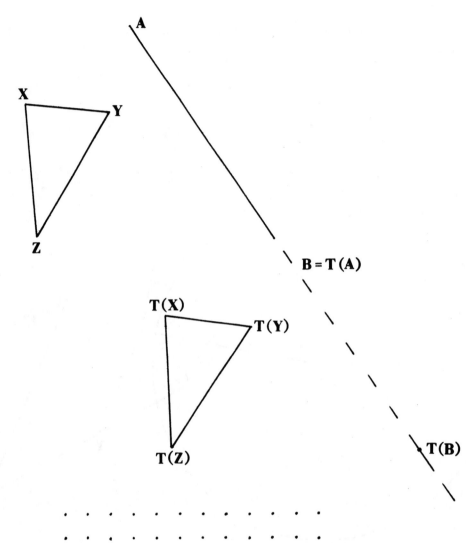

2.4

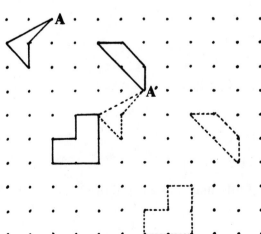

2.5 ⊙A′ and ⊙B intersect at B′.

⊙C and $\overleftrightarrow{AA'}$ intersect at C′.

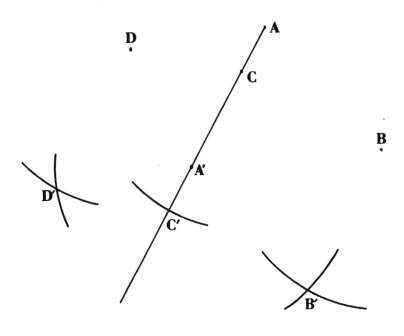

2.6

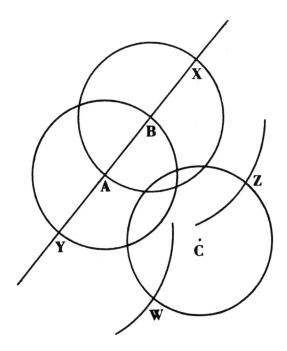

2.7 The lines l, m, and q are parallel.

2.8 Note that T(F(P)) = F(T(P))

2.9 $F(\triangle X'Y'Z') = F(T(\triangle XYZ)) = F \circ T(\triangle XYZ)$.

$T(\triangle X''Y''Z'') = T(F(\triangle XYZ)) = T \circ F(\triangle XYZ)$.

$F \circ T(\triangle XYZ)$ and $T \circ F(\triangle XYZ)$ should coincide.

2.10 $T \circ F$ maps B onto $T(B')$ and maps A onto $F(A')$.

Remember that $T \circ F = F \circ T$.

$T \circ F$ is the translation G defined by $G(X) = T(F(X)) = F(T(X))$.

2.12 Exercises (a) and (b) demonstrate that rotations preserve distance and angle measure.
That is, if A' is the image of A, B' is the image of B, and C' is the image of C, then
AB = A'B', AC = A'C', BC = B'C', $m\angle ABC = m\angle A'B'C'$, $m\angle BAC = m\angle B'A'C'$, and
$m\angle ACB = m\angle A'C'B'$. The image of O is O, so OA = O'A', OB = O'B', and OC = O'C'.
The measure of the angle of rotation is $m\angle AOA' = m\angle BOB' = m\angle COC'$.
$AA' \neq BB' \neq CC'$.

Compare these properties with the translation properties in exercise 2.2.

2.13 In exercise 2.12 you found that the distance between a point and its image is not
constant under a rotation.

However, if O is the center of the rotation and two points, A and B, are on a circle
with center O, then AA' = BB'.

2.14 Lines p, q, and s are concurrent at C.

2.15 Draw the perpendicular bisector m of $\overline{XX'}$ and the perpendicular bisector n of $\overline{YY'}$.
The center of the rotation R is $m \cap n$.

2.16

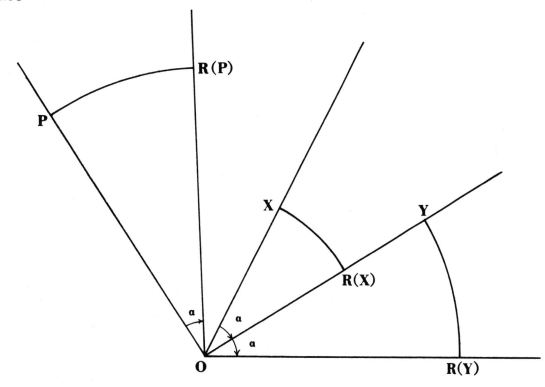

2.17

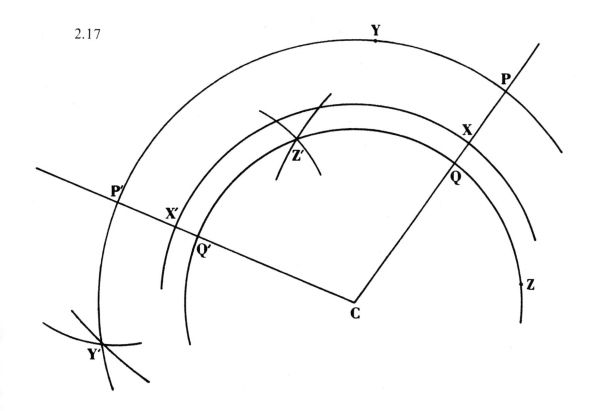

2.19   Choose any point G on the island.

Find the image P of G under a 90° counterclockwise rotation about A and find

the image Q of G under a clockwise 90° rotation about B.

Then the midpoint C of $\overline{PQ}$ is the point so that CAB is a right isosceles triangle

with AC = BC.

2.20   This is an application of half-turns.

Michael goes home.

2.21   Draw ⊙C with radius CP.

Let ⊙C intersect the rays of the given angles at Z, Y, W, and V, as indicated below.

Note that $Y = R_\beta(Z)$ and $V = R_\alpha(W)$.

Draw ⊙Y with radius ZP or draw ⊙P with radius YZ to locate $P' = R_\beta(P)$.

Draw ⊙V with radius P'W or draw ⊙P' with radius WV to locate $P'' = R_\alpha(P') =$

$R_\alpha(R_\beta(P)) = R_\alpha \circ R_\beta(P)$.

m∠PCP' = β and m∠P'CP'' = α, so m∠PCP'' = $\beta + \alpha$.

Try similar exercises where one rotation is clockwise and the other counterclockwise.

Also locate the image of a point under $R_1 \circ R_2$ and $R_2 \circ R_1$ where R_1 and R_2 are

rotations with different centers.

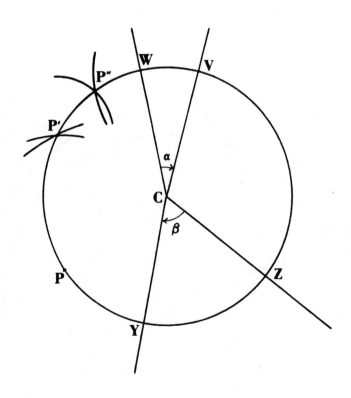

2.23 $R_a \circ R_\beta$ maps any point X onto $R_a(R_\beta(X)) = X''$.

X'' is on the circle with center C and radius CX, so X'' must be the image of X

under a rotation with center C.

$m\angle XCX'' = \beta + a$, so the measure of the rotation is $\beta + a$.

Describe the rotation $R_a \circ R_\beta$ where one is clockwise and the other counterclockwise.

2.29 If $r_m(A) = A'$ and $r_m(B) = B'$, then:

   (a) $r_m(\overline{AB}) = \overline{A'B'}$

   (b) $r_m(\overleftrightarrow{AB}) = \overleftrightarrow{A'B'}$

   (c) $r_m(\overrightarrow{AB}) = \overrightarrow{A'B'}$.

2.30 $r_m(\overline{AC}) \cap r_m(\overline{DE}) = r_m(\overline{AC} \cap \overline{DE}) = r_m(B)$.

$r_m(\overline{AC}) \cap m = r_m(\overline{AC} \cap m) = F$.

Note that $r_m(m) = m$.

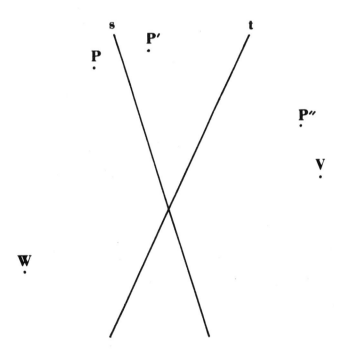

P' = $r_s(P)$, P'' = $r_t \circ r_s(P) = r_t(P')$, V = $r_t(P)$, W = $r_s \circ r_t(P) = r_s(V)$.

2.33 If $p \perp q$, then $r_p \circ r_q = r_q \circ r_p$.

If $p = q$, then $r_p \circ r_q(P) = P$ for every point P of the plane; that is, $r_p \circ r_q$ is the

identity transformation.

2.34   The center O of the rotation R is the point common to the perpendicular bisectors of $\overline{AA'}$, $\overline{BB'}$, and $\overline{CC'}$.

To locate p and q, draw any line q through the center of the rotation. So you may choose one of the perpendicular bisectors of $\overline{AA'}$, $\overline{BB'}$, or $\overline{CC'}$.

Locate r_q ($\triangle ABC$), and then find the Mira line p that reflects r_q ($\triangle ABC$) onto $\triangle A'B'C'$.

The measure of the angle of rotation is $m\angle AOA' = m\angle BOB' = m\angle COC'$.

The measure of the acute angle between p and q is one-half the measure of the angle of rotation.

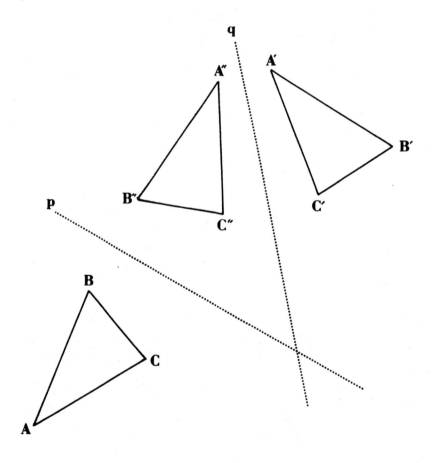

2.35   Let $p \cap q = C$ and let θ denote the measure of the acute angle between p and q. Then R is the counterclockwise rotation with center C. The measure of the angle of rotation is 2θ.

160

2.37   Choose any line t so that t is perpendicular to $\overleftrightarrow{PP'}$. Locate r_t ($\triangle PQR$), and then find the Mira line s that reflects r_t ($\triangle PQR$) onto $\triangle P'Q'R'$.

The distance between s and t is one-half the distance between a point and its image.

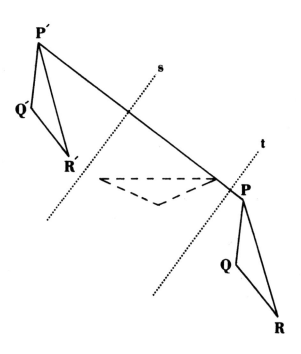

2.39   Locate:

    (a) $\triangle A'B'C' = r_t$ ($\triangle ABC$)

    (b) $\triangle A''B''C'' = r_q$ ($\triangle A'B'C'$)

    (c) $\triangle A'''B'''C''' = r_p$ ($\triangle A''B''C''$).

The find the Mira line s that reflects $\triangle ABC$ onto $\triangle A'''B'''C'''$.

2.40   Since t‖p, $r_t \circ r_p$ is a translation T.

The points A″, B″, and C″ are on s.

2.41

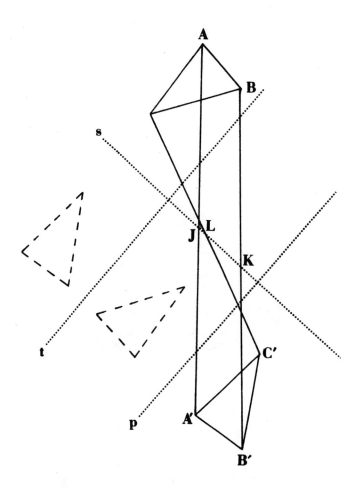

2.42   Locate:

        (a) $\triangle X'Y'Z' = r_s(\triangle XYZ)$

        (b) $\triangle X''Y''Z'' = r_p(\triangle X'Y'Z')$

        (c) $\triangle X'''Y'''Z''' = r_t(\triangle X''Y''Z'')$.

Then find the Mira Line that reflects $\triangle XYZ$ onto $\triangle X'''Y'''Z'''$.

2.43   Locate $\triangle X'Y'Z' = r_q \circ r_p \circ r_q(\triangle XYZ)$. Then m is the perpendicular bisector of $\overline{XX'}$.

Locate $\triangle X''Y''Z'' = r_p \circ r_q \circ r_p(\triangle XYZ)$. Then n is the perpendicular bisector of $\overline{XX''}$.

$r_q \circ r_q(P) = P$ for every point in the plane, so $r_q \circ r_q = I$, the identity transformation.

If G is any transformation, then $G \circ I = I = I \circ G$.

So $r_p \circ r_q \circ r_q = r_p \circ I = r_p = I \circ r_p = r_q \circ r_q \circ r_p$.

Note: Reflections reverse orientation. Orientation is preserved under the composite of two reflections. Orientation is reversed under the composite of three reflections.

2.44   The isometry $r_k \circ r_j$ is a translation since $k \parallel j$. Translations preserve parallelism and distance, so the isometry $r_{k'} \circ r_{j'} = r_k \circ r_j$.
This exercise shows that if $k \parallel j$ and if k' and j' are the images of k and j under a translation, then $r_k \circ r_j = r_{k'} \circ r_{j'}$.

2.45   The isometry $r_p \circ r_q$ is a rotation since p and q are two distinct nonparallel lines. The measure of the angle of the rotation R' is twice the measure of the angle between p and q. Rotations preserve angle measure and $R(C) = C$, so the isometry $r_{p'} \circ r_{q'} = r_p \circ r_q$. This exercise demonstrates that if $p \cap q = C$ and p' and q' are the images of p and q under any rotation with center C, then $r_p \circ r_q = r_{p'} \circ r_{q'}$.

2.46   Let a denote the measure of the acute angle between b and c. Then the clockwise rotation R with center P and rotation angle of measure a maps b onto c. That is, $R(b) = c$. Note that if m is the midline of b and c, then, $r_c \circ r_m = r_m \circ r_b = R$. Locate $a' = R(a)$. Since $R(b) = c$ and $R(a) = a'$, we know from exercise 2.45 that $r_a \circ r_b = r_{a'} \circ r_c$. So $r_a \circ r_b \circ r_c = r_{a'} \circ r_c \circ r_c$. But $r_c \circ r_c = I$, the identity transformation. Therefore, $r_a \circ r_b \circ r_c = r_{a'} \circ I = r_{a'}$. Thus, an isometry which is a composite of three reflections over concurrent lines is a reflection.

2.47   If A is any point on p and B is any point on s, then the translation defined by

T(A) = B maps p onto s. That is, T(p) = s.

Let n be the line through B so that $n \perp \overline{AB}$ and let m be the perpendicular bisector

of $\overline{AB}$. Then $T = r_n \circ r_m$.

Locate $q' = T(q)$.

Since T(p) = s and T(q) = q', we know from exercise 2.44 that $r_q \circ r_p = r_{q'} \circ r_s$.

So $r_q \circ r_p \circ r_s = r_{q'} \circ r_s \circ r_s$.

But $r_s \circ r_s = I$, the identity transformation, so $r_q \circ r_p \circ r_s = r_{q'} \circ I = r_{q'}$.

Hence, an isometry which is a composite of three reflections about parallel lines

is a reflection.

2.48   Choose any point X on p and draw the line p' through X so that $p' \perp q$. You could

choose $X = p \cap q$.

Let θ be the measure of the acute angle between p and p'.

Then R is the rotation with center X and rotation angle of measure θ. The

direction of R will depend on the location of p. In this example, R is

counterclockwise.

Let m be the midline of p' and p.

Then $r_{p'} \circ r_m = r_m \circ r_p = R$.

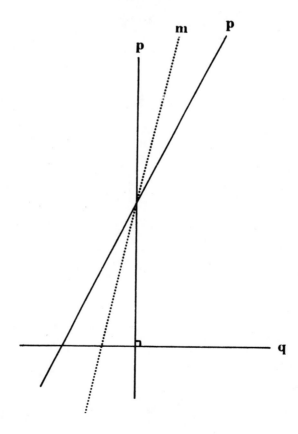

2.49   From Exercise 2.45 we know that if we choose any rotation with center

$X = p \cap s$, then $r_{p'} \circ r_{s'} = r_p \circ r_s$. So as in the previous exercise, draw the line s'

through X so that $s' \perp q$. Then let R be the rotation with center X and with

measure of rotation angle equal to the measure of the acute angle between

s and s' $(R = r_{s'} \circ r_m)$. Then $R(s) = s'$, $s' \perp q$, and $r_p \circ r_s = r_{p'} \circ r_{s'}$.

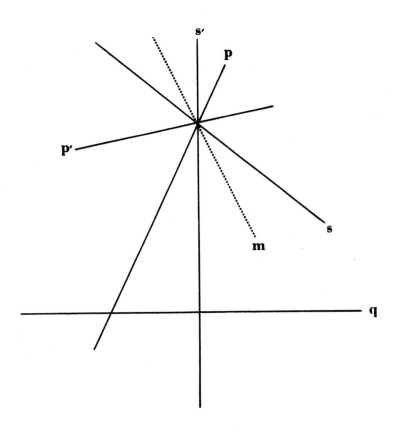

2.50   Let $Y = s \cap t$ and draw the line s' through Y so that $s' \| p$.

Let a denote the measure of the acute angle between s and s'.

If R is the counterclockwise rotation with center Y and rotation angle of measure

a, R maps s to s'. That is, $R(s) = s'$.

Locate $t' = R(t)$.

$t' \perp s'$ and $s' \| p$. Therefore $t' \perp p$.

Hence the isometry $r_{t'} \circ r_{s'} \circ r_p = r_t \circ r_s \circ r_p$ is a glide reflection.

2.51   Draw the line b' through $X = a \cap b$ so that $b' \perp c$. Let m be a midline of b and b'. Then $R_1 = r_{b'} \circ r_m$. Locate $a' = R(a)$. Draw the line b'' through $Y = b' \cap c$ so that $b'' \parallel a'$. Let n be a midline of b' and b''. Then $R_2 = r_{b''} \circ r_n$. Locate $c' = R(c)$. The center of the rotation R_1 is $X = a \cap b$, so $r_b \circ r_a = r_{b'} \circ r_{a'}$. The center of the rotation R_2 is $Y = b' \cap c$, so $r_c \circ r_{b'} = r_{c'} \circ r_{b''}$. Hence, $r_c \circ r_b \circ r_a = r_c \circ r_{b'} \circ r_{a'} = r_{c'} \circ r_{b''} \circ r_{a'}$. $b'' \perp c'$, since $b' \perp c$. $b'' \parallel a'$. So $c' \perp a'$. Therefore the isometry $r_{c'} \circ r_{b''} \circ r_{a'}$ is a glide reflection.

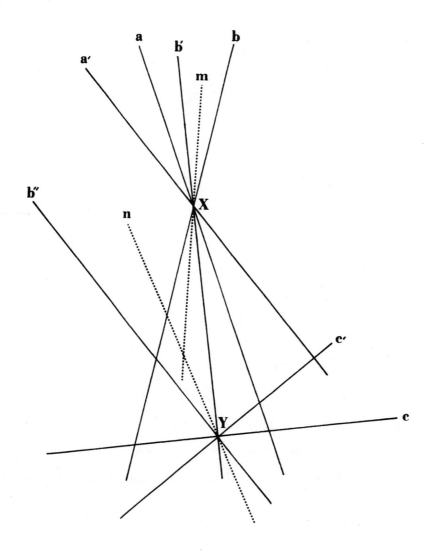

Note: If $a \cap b \neq b \cap c$, then the composite $r_c \circ r_b \circ r_a$ is a glide reflection.

2.52   The images of X, Y, and Z under $r_c \circ r_b \circ r_a$ are X′, Y′, and Z′,

respectively. That is, $r_c \circ r_b \circ r_a$ (△XYZ) = △X′Y′Z′.

Since $a \cap b \neq b \cap c$, $r_c \circ r_b \circ r_a$ is a glide reflection.

Locate a′, b″, and c′ as in the previous exercise.

Locate the midpoints of $\overline{XX'}$, $\overline{YY'}$, and $\overline{ZZ'}$. Refer to Exercise 2.41.

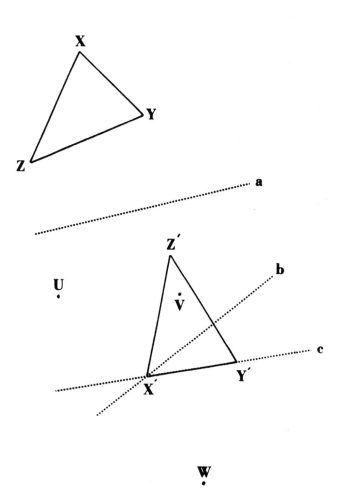

$U = r_a(Z)$, $V = r_a(Y)$, $W = r_b(r_a(Z))$.

2.53   An isometry S such that S(P) = P is called an isometry with a fixed point.
The distance between P and S(B) must equal the distance between P and B;
and the distance between A' = S(A) and S(B) must equal the distance
between A and B. So S(B) must be on ⊙P with radius BP and on ⊙A' with
radius AB. Thus there are only two possibilities for S(B). Refer to the
diagram. If S(B) = B', then S is a reflection. If S(B) = B'', then S is a rotation.
These are the only two possibilities for S. Hence if S is an isometry with a
fixed point, then S is a reflection or a rotation.

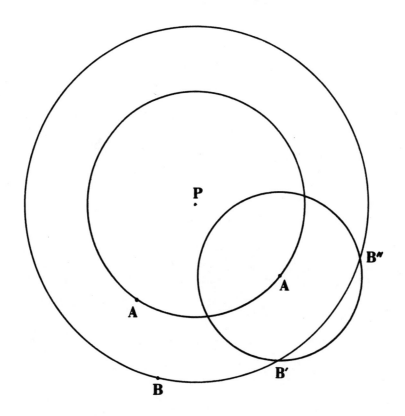

2.54 M(A) = A′ and A ≠ A′ since M has no fixed point.

Since p is the perpendicular bisector of $\overline{AA'}$, r_p (A′) = A.

Therefore $r_p \circ M(A) = r_p(M(A)) = r_p(A') = A$. That is, $r_p \circ M$ is an isometry with a fixed point, and from the previous exercise we know that $r_p \circ M$ is a reflection or a rotation.

Since $r_p \circ r_p \circ M = M$, M is the composite of two reflections or the composite of a reflection and a rotation. But a rotation is the composite of two reflections. So M is the composite of two reflections or the composite of three reflections.

2.55 Example B is an isometry; namely, a half-turn.

2.56 $\overleftrightarrow{AA'}$, $\overleftrightarrow{BB'}$, and $\overleftrightarrow{CC'}$ are concurrent.

2.57 $\overline{PY} \parallel \overline{QY'}$.

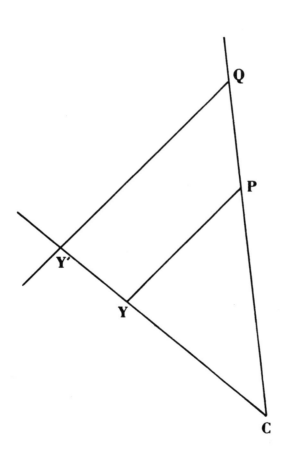

2.59 $\overline{PS} \parallel \overline{QS'}$ and $\overline{ST} \parallel \overline{S'T'}$.

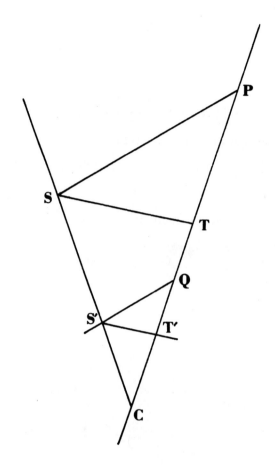

2.60 $\overline{PJ} \parallel \overline{QJ'}$ and $\overline{JK} \parallel \overline{J'K'}$.

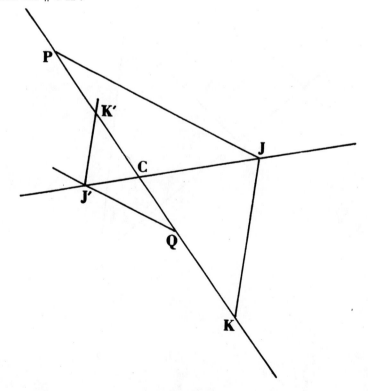

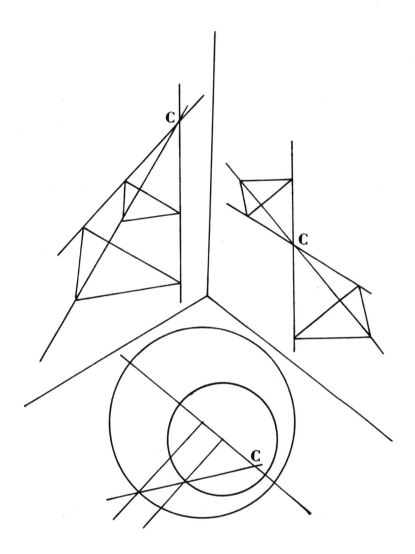

2.62   The isometry that maps ∠ABC onto ∠A′YX is the rotation $r_n \circ r_m$. The size transformation that maps △A′YX onto △A′B′C′ is $D_{A′,X,C′}$. That is $D_{A′,X,C′} \circ r_n \circ r_m(\triangle ABC) = \triangle A′B′C′$.

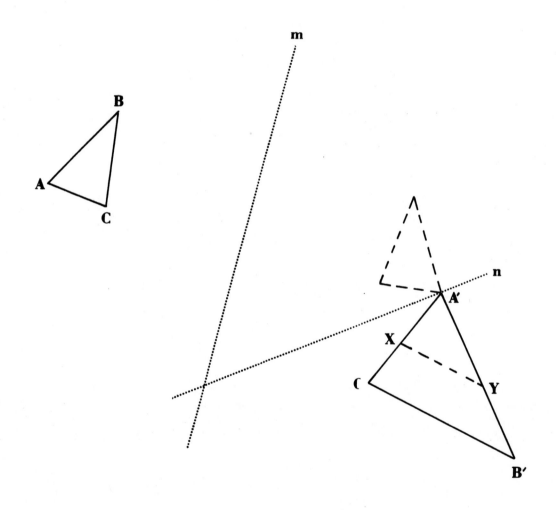